The Management of Service Business

Second Edition

Contact:

christian.m.wegner@web.de

http://linkedin.com/in/christian-m-wegner-852012123

http://twitter.com/ChrisWegner99

Bibliografische Information der Deutschen Nationalbibliothek: Die Deutsche Nationalbibliothek verzeichnet diese Publika in der Deutschen Nationalbibliografie; detaillierte bibliografische Daten sind im Internet über dnb.dnb.de abrufbar.

Herstellung und Verlag: BoD – Books on Demand, Norderstedt

ISBN: 978-3-759-71356-8

This book is also available in e-book format.

Contents

Personal Note

After finishing my studies in electrical engineering, I dreamed of a technical career in the development of large electrical machines like big motors, generators and transformers. Yet, by chance my first professional engagement was in service. I started as a service engineer for industrial computers in a large electrical company. In the beginning, I was a little bit disappointed because, compared to engineering, I considered service a less attractive area of activity. During the first couple of years, I was filled with doubt whether I have made the right professional choice. The confirmation that this was the best choice I could ever have made came only slowly. Our computers were in charge of controlling complex industrial processes, such as in steel mills, coal mines, or power plants. Therefore, their reliable function was mission-critical for the business success of our customers, and each fault would have had severe consequences. Each time I was able to solve a problem, it made me proud, and seeing the relief of our customers once their operation was restored gave me a strong sense of purpose. Troubleshooting is a special capability which can be acquired especially in service. It requires a high degree of analytical thinking, creativity, and pragmatism. Finding a sporadic error in the source code of an operation system is difficult. Finding it during live operation and under the menace of possibly stopping a several hundred million Euro installation is even more challenging. I cannot think of any area of technical activity better suited for young people for learning to deal with pressure and to assume responsibility than service.

Later, after starting in managing a service business, I learned that service is a people's business, and therefore, the human factor is of decisive relevance. In large service projects, like the integral service for the logistic systems of a major airport, a couple of hundred people may be engaged. Aligning them toward the common goal of ensuring the success of their customer is a demanding management task requiring empathy and strong social skills. More than in any other business, being successful in service means loving to work with people, trusting them, and giving them a strong sense of purpose.

Sharing business success with all the service people in my organization was the most rewarding aspect of my career. I owe them my genuine gratitude.

Christian M. Wegner

October, 2023

Preface

Technical service is a large business field. It ranges from selling spare parts to the integral asset management of large installations. Many people think: "Service is just service." This assumption is wrong. Each type of service has its own rules and its specific success factors. Many people also think that service is a simple residue of the systems business and comes automatically. This assumption is also wrong. Developing service to a sustainable and profitable business of relevant size requires a strategic life-cycle orientation of the company. It also requires talented and dedicated service managers with a wide range of skills including technical, social, intercultural, and entrepreneurial ones. Only few systems and installations companies succeed in maximizing their capitalization on the service opportunities stemming from their products, systems, and installations. For these companies, recognizing the special strategic relevance of service and regarding it as an equally important business pillar as systems and installations is a key success factor. In markets in which customers predominantly outsource the technical services for their systems, successful installations companies generate up to 30% of their revenues through service.

Covering all aspects of such a large area of activity in one attempt would be confusing. Thus, any discussion about service must focus on one specific type of this business. Basic services, like, for example, spare parts supply and on-call support, are already well covered in technical literature. There is also a lot of information available about various technical aspects of service, such as condition monitoring, failure analysis and maintenance planning. On the other side, subject matter books and articles about the management of a business offering complex technical services for large installations (like the integral maintenance and technical operation) are hard to find. Therefore, this book focuses on various managing aspects related especially to this kind of business and primarily addresses managers of service. Even though written mainly from the perspective of an integrated service supplier of a systems and installations company, the book contains valuable information also for generic service companies and for customers who operate large technical installations and need to service them.

All terms marked in the following with an asterisk (*) are summarized and shortly explained in the Glossary at the end of this book.

Chapter Overview

In the **General Considerations** chapter, the book addresses the increasing relevance of the service business for systems and installations companies. Those companies succeeding in establishing service as an equally important business pillar in addition to their systems business and thus in capitalizing maximally on the service opportunities yielded by their installations will be more successful—both in terms of enhanced financial performance and customer retention.
The chapter explains the nature of the service business, talks about success factors, and introduces and explains a couple of subject-matter terms which are used in the following of this book. It explains why service requires a specific business culture and why in service, as a people's business, committed and dedicated people are the most valuable business asset. It further introduces the main focus of this book—the service business for large systems and installations.

Service Types explains the difference between *support services* and *strategic services* and introduces the different service types in the context of a reference service portfolio of a mature systems and installations company. It further explains on which activities systems and installations companies should have their main focus and emphasizes the relevance of an integral service approach including also the modernization of systems.

Strategy and Tactics explains these two important business terms and shows how they should be used to manage the development of service business. It shows why it is imperative that the service strategy of a systems and installations company must cover both the *growth* as well as the *protection* aspects of its service business. It further explains the interdependence between the new systems and the service business and shows how these two areas must be aligned to maximize the global business success. The chapter also highlights the relevance of a consistent life-cycle approach of systems and installations companies.

The **Planning** chapter starts by breaking with a couple of erroneous paradigms which still prevail regarding the profitability expectations for service. It then explains how the *service market* works and how it must be assessed. It shows why the structure of the service market is different from the new systems one and why these two markets follow different rules and have a different development.
It then describes how, on the basis of a sound market assessment, *new orders* and *sales* should be planned. It further introduces a couple of *business indicators* used to monitor the development of the service business.
In its last part, the chapter explains why *profit planning* is closely linked to *risk management* and *continuous improvement.*

Sales presents the most relevant specific sales success factors for each kind of service. It explains why selling *support services* is very different from selling *strategic services* and shows why for the latter the engagement of the top management of service companies is essential for winning a large service contract. It explains why developing a smart individual tactical approach for each large service project is an important prerequisite and emphasizes the relevance of a proper internal alignment between the new systems and the services divisions of systems and installations companies. The chapter addresses some typical scenarios in the sales process of large service contracts and gives a couple of practical hints for overcoming difficult situations during contract negotiation.

The **Competition** chapter describes how and why the competitive landscape differs significantly between the new systems and the service business of systems and installations companies. It emphasizes the strong competitive position of their internal service division for acquiring the service for new installations. The chapter gives valuable hints with regard to how service suppliers can enhance their competitive position and retain their contracts. It also provides help for structuring service contracts and shows how smart pricing can increase the chances for winning such a contract.

Contracts starts with an overview of the different contract types used in the service for systems and installations. It then introduces the most important *performance indicators* and gives advice with regard to how these indicators can be used and combined to form a meaningful performance scheme. This chapter also focuses on the *liability of suppliers* in service contracts and shows how suppliers and customers can agree on fair and target-orientated terms to the benefit of both parties. It explains the different liability terms in detail and shows how these are handled in practice. In the end, the chapter addresses the strongly disputed issue between customers and suppliers regarding the handling of *inflation* in long-term contracts.

Customer Relationship shows why, more than in any other technical business, maintaining a good relationship with their customers is mission-critical for business success of service companies. It explains how a good customer relationship can be established at operational, site management, and top management level and why it is important that *customer relationship* *management (CRM)* must include all these three levels. It underlines the high importance of assessing the *customer satisfaction* on a regular basis and gives practical hints for carrying out such an assessment in large service projects.

The **Operations** chapter explains why in a successful service contract active *contract management* is indispensable. It presents the main objectives of contract management and introduces the three basic elements of service excellence: *organizational efficiency*, *operational effectiveness*, and *continuous improvement*. The chapter ends with showing why *contract development* is a mandatory task for ensuring the long-term sustainability of the service business.

Supplier Maturity presents a couple of criteria which customers can use for selecting the appropriate service provider and introduces the concept of a *maturity sphere* for service providers. It explains which prerequisites service providers must fulfill to become genuine life-cycle partners of their customers.

In the **International Business** chapter, the book focuses on the special challenges service providers are faced with in the process of setting up an international presence. Many large customers have international sites, and following these customers around the world requires special preparation. The chapter also introduces the management practices required for developing and controlling an international service business.

Technology and Innovation provides a guideline for introducing new technical developments in service projects and addresses a couple of pitfalls service providers may fall into in this regard. It emphasizes the importance of making sure that all technical and technological innovations in service projects must always rely on a solid financial justification.

The Value of Service chapter introduces a methodology for determining the value of good service along its three main goals: (1) ensuring the safe and reliable operation of the installation; (2) preserving the installation in good technical condition; (3) adapting the installation to changing operational and technical requirements. By using an example from the airport logistics, it demonstrates how this value can be translated into real financial terms. For customers, this information is of great importance in the selection process of the appropriate service provider. For service providers, it presents the essential arguments for avoiding a pure price-based debate (favored by the purchasing departments of customers) and for conducting contract negotiations in a value-based manner.
Because the three above-mentioned service goals are always the same in the installations business, this methodology maintains its validity across other industries.

In the **Business Valuation** chapter, the book provides a methodology for calculating the fair market value of a service company in the installations business by presenting two concrete examples. The first example addresses the valuation of an integrated service supplier as part of the total business of an installations company. The second one deals with the valuation of a stand-alone generic service provider. The chapter also addresses in detail potential risks related to the acquisition of such a business. Thus, it is providing comprehensive information for making sound buying decisions.

General Considerations

Not long ago, most ***systems and installations companies****
perceived service as an unpleasant duty and were happy not to hear anything from their customers again once their installations went into operation. Possibly, these companies were earning some low hanging fruits in the area of service by selling spare parts, hot-line, and on-call support. These basic services usually brought in good money and required little effort. Service was regarded as a secondary, low priority business, usually receiving little management attention.

Over the last three decades, more and more companies discovered the strategic and operational relevance of maintaining a sustained presence during the entire life cycle of their systems and installations. At the same time, a growing number of customers started asking themselves whether the maintenance of their technical assets had to be considered a core activity executed by own resources or rather be regarded as a non-core area which could be outsourced to external service supplies. As a result, new services such as Operation and Maintenance (O&M) and also new companies specialized on these services emerged. Most of today's large systems and installations companies have set up own large service units offering their customers (the system owners or operators) a broad spectrum of technical services along the entire life cycle of their systems. In the following, service departments of systems and installations companies will be called ***integrated service suppliers****. Additionally, there are also many ***generic services providers****
in the service market who are specialized only on service and do not have an own systems business. Most of them are usually

smaller and locally acting companies of lower technological profile.

For systems and installations companies, staying engaged during the entire life cycle of their systems has many advantages. O&M contracts run over a longer period of time and are generating a continuous revenue stream. The on-site presence of own service personnel during the first years of operation makes the warranty process more efficient by ensuring a better service for the customer at less costs for the supplier. Suppliers can gain important information about the long-term behavior of their systems, which they can use to improve their new products. Furthermore, the need for system upgrading and modernization yields good opportunities for additional business. Quality service is also an important factor for high customer satisfaction and thus customer retention.

Servicing technical systems is something very different form manufacturing and installing them. Thus, to be successful, this business requires service specialists and service managers. Interestingly, vocational education still does not have service management in its focus. Just a few universities offer service courses. Because service has still little exposure when companies compete for new talents, young people generally perceive it as less challenging and less attractive in comparison with the product or installations business. This impression is false though. Especially for young people at the beginning of a management career, service offers an interesting combination of technical and people-related aspects. Primarily a people's business, service opens unique opportunities for developing skills in the area of leadership and organization. As service takes place during the operational phase of systems, when these systems must produce customer value and when downtime means loss of production and profits, service is a business requiring decision making capabilities, responsibility, and entrepreneurial spirit.

Because it does not require significant investments, service is one of the businesses with the highest return on assets. The costs for the recruiting and training of service people are usually the only larger upfront expenditures. The main resource needed in service are people. Therefore, organizational efficiency is a decisive success factor in this business.

A specific risk factor of service is related to personnel. This risk can be relevant especially when large service contracts cannot be renewed, and thus service people possibly need to be terminated. Even though requiring certain attention, this residual personnel risk is often overrated. Well trained service people who are accustomed with a specific installation are extremely valuable. Most times in such a case, the new contractor or the customer would be happy to take over these people. In some countries, this is even mandatory according to the local labor law.

Thinking that 'service is just service' is the cause of many management mistakes. Service is a vast field with a large variety of different businesses following their own rules. Simply extrapolating experiences gathered in one area of service activity to another will not yield the expected results.

Generally, **product and small systems service** is a combination of on-call service, maintenance support, and spare parts supply. These technical services are quite straight forward and already well described in subject matter literature. Therefore, as a matter of completeness, they will be touched only briefly in the following.

An efficient *spare parts supply* is a mandatory prerequisite for all mature product, systems, and installations companies. Predictable delivery times and the availability of (also older) spare parts are the most important quality parameters in this kind of business. In this regard, predictable does not necessarily mean short. Making certain parts available may take some time, but if this duration is predictable, customers can well define their individual spare parts strategies in accordance with the procurement lead times and the criticality of their systems. Many suppliers have automated the order process by offering their customers on-line access to their digital spare parts internet portals. Spare parts contracts usually include contractual obligations, such as delivery times and the guaranteed availability of critical parts, which, if breached, may trigger penalties.

O*n-call service* ensures the technical support of specialists of the supplier in the event of system failures. It usually comprises two or three escalation levels. Usually, the first level service is carried out by the customer's own operational or maintenance people. This includes basic activities like inspections and simple troubleshooting. For more complex problems, the second service level is activated by calling the supplier's hot-line. This service is usually provided by technicians of the supplier, often located in a service point in the greater area. High-end service activities, such a finding a sporadic failure in a complex system, are carried out by specialists of the supplier from a central service department. Sometimes, service levels two and three can be combined.

Maintenance support comprises the regular execution of certain maintenance tasks for which the customer's service technicians do not have the required level of expertise and therefore the engagement of service specialists of the supplier is needed.

On-call service and maintenance support can be very efficient if the products and systems are capable of producing meaningful diagnostic data and allow that certain activities can be carried out on-line. The availability of such embedded technical features allows a much faster reaction in the case of failures and thus helps to significantly reduce their consequences. Additionally, saving travel time reduces costs and makes service more cost-effective. With the support of remote diagnostics and maintenance, a few well trained technicians can efficiently service a large base of distributed systems. As critical systems require strict compliance with contractually agreed reaction and sometimes even restoration times, managers have to carefully determine the number of required technicians. Having not enough people may result in the non-fulfillment of contractual obligations, especially when more technical incidents require attendance at the same time. Employing too many people results in excessive costs. Correctly assessing the operational and contractual risks and finding the right balance regarding the use of resources are the big challenges in this type of business.

Managing a business related to the **integral service for large systems and installations** is a different matter. Unlike on-call service and spare parts supply, this kind of service is poorly covered by technical literature.
Large installations, like industrial plants, airport logistic systems, or power plants, are generally serviced by ***resident (on-site) service organizations****. If these services are outsourced, they are rendered either by integrated service suppliers or by generic service providers. As these service activities are closely linked to the system operation and take place inside the installations premises, service providers become integral part of their customers' business. Thus, they have a decisive role in ensuring the overall business success of their clients.

The success of service for large installations depends on many aspects of different nature.

To generate profit, service must be efficient. Efficiency is defined as *result* divided by *effort*. In service, being efficient means producing the best possible technical result by using the least possible amount of (human) resources—in other words, highest possible effectiveness at lowest possible costs.

Service effectiveness means producing a good technical result, for example high equipment availability and reliability. It is not only determined by technical aspects, such as the right maintenance strategy, appropriate maintenance methods, and good service tools, but is also closely related to the skills level of service technicians.

Lowest possible effort and lowest possible costs are the result of an appropriate organizational set-up and of clear processes, including good work management and the smart distribution of people in the installation.

High service efficiency is closely linked to continuous improvement and requires the active engagement of all employees. Continuous improvement is the result of a collective effort, and thus an important aspect of business culture.
Implementing a positive business culture at project level is mission-critical for the success of resident services for large installations. People need to be motivated to constantly reflect about what they do and to think about what they can improve. Motivating higher skilled people, who usually also receive higher salaries, is already sometimes challenging. In this kind of projects, the majority of the workforce is made up by people with a lower level of professional education. Many of them are

executing rather simple and recurring maintenance tasks and are receiving a comparatively moderate pay. Motivating these people is even more challenging and requires a sustained management effort. This is not only a question of adequate remuneration but also a matter of recognition and respect.

This business requires service managers with a high level of social competence. This skill is not only necessary with regard to the own people but is also very important in the direction of customers. Living together with the customer under the same roof is not always easy. It lies in the nature of this business that occasional disputes with the customer are unavoidable. In such situations, service managers should avoid an escalation and must find smart ways to calm down the situation. Social competence is not only required from the managers. It is also important that good cooperation is ensured at all operational levels down to shop floor. Service people must be sensitized to adopt a respectful attitude towards their peers on the customer side and to establish a trustful working relationship.

Resident service for large installations is a complex business with many facets, far beyond of just mastering technical challenges. Smart work management, organizational efficiency, people management, legal savvy, and social and intercultural intelligence are further decisive success factors in this business.

From the business perspective of an external service provider, the ***outsourcing maturity**** of the respective industry is of major importance. The decision for the outsourcing of services is of strategic relevance and is usually made at the executive level of companies. In an outsourcing-friendly market, the majority of the customers prefer to engage external service partners for servicing their systems. In these markets, service suppliers have the opportunity for providing comprehensive services such as the ***integral O&M**** of systems. A good example for such a market environment is airport logistics (baggage and cargo handling systems). In other industries, such as automotive, in-house service departments prevail, and only few services are executed by external partners. In this case the service coverage of external suppliers is significantly lower.

Service Types

There are several different types of service which can be categorized into the following two main groups:

- Strategic services, also called business oriented services

  These services are of strategic relevance for the customer, and determining the way they are organized requires the engagement of the company's top management in the decision making. For example, the CEO or COO of a company decide whether the integral service for a critical system is sourced out or is executed in-house. Operation and Maintenance (O&M) and large modernization projects fall into this category.

- Support services, also called operational services

  These are services geared at supporting the ***in-house service organizations***[*] of customers. Decisions regarding the execution of these services are usually made at the level of the customer's maintenance manager. This category comprises planned maintenance, on-call service, spare parts supply, and smaller modernization projects.

For mature integrated service suppliers operating in an outsourcing-friendly market segment, a benchmark for the business split could be set as follows:

70% Operation and Maintenance (O&M): Comprises the integral maintenance and technical operation of large systems. This kind of service is rendered by resident (on-site) service organizations. Spare parts supply is usually integral part of such contracts.

This segment is the business backbone. The chances for the system suppliers to be also awarded the service for a new installation are high. Therefore, it is essential for the success of their business that integrated service suppliers acquire the vast majority of service contracts for their own new systems, at least for the initial period of two to five years. The only acceptable reason for not succeeding in this regard would be a customer's decision to service his systems with own resources. For customers, ramping up an own service organization, finding suitable people for the technical areas of higher complexity, and ensuring the required knowledge transfer from the supplier is often quite difficult. Especially for complex systems, the operational risk is significantly reduced if the supplier also takes over the service. Outsourcing also simplifies warranty issues. In most cases, the customers will outsource the services for their systems if the supplier is capable of making an attractive service offer. Therefore, it is especially not acceptable losing such a contract to competition. If suppliers fail in acquiring the service by the time when the system goes into operation, this opportunity will never come back. The loss of such a project is usually the result of poor performance during system installation or of a bad job in the preparation of the service offer.

Many service managers spend too much time searching for opportunities in the old installed base of own systems. This is usually wasted effort. The entry barriers are high. Customers may be servicing their systems with own people or may have outsourced the service to a cheap local service provider. They probably also have found alternative sources for the procurement of all non-proprietary spare parts.

10% Maintenance Support and On-call Service: Comprises regular maintenance activities and sporadic interventions in the event of system failure.

These services are geared at supporting the own service organizations of customers and usually comprise activities requiring higher qualifications than the customers can afford to keep in their own service organizations.

Some customers have a clear in-house service strategy—either because they do not want to be dependent on another party or because they consider their operation too critical for giving the entire service into the hands of external suppliers. Still, it is very important for the suppliers to maintain their presence in the life cycle of their systems. For many customers, keeping own specialists for hi-tech systems, such as automation and IT, is expensive and may also result in an under-utilization of these personnel resources. Therefore, it is more economical to receive these services from external providers. Thus, integrated service suppliers have a good opportunity for acquiring long-term support contracts.

15% Modernization: Comprises system refurbishment, upgrade, rehabilitation, and performance increase.

By taking an active part in the life cycle of systems, service suppliers are always in pole position regarding the acquisition of modernization jobs. They know the system, how it performs, and where potential weaknesses could impair operation, and they also can anticipate when and which components may become obsolete. Usually, the initial system design reflects certain operational conditions and performance requirements at the beginning of operation. These requirements may change in time, and the system may become unsuitable to optimally fulfill them. Modernization projects are always targeted at one of the following three goals: (1) reducing the operational risk, like from unplanned system downtime and obsolete components; (2) avoiding cost driving factors, such as proprietary and maintenance-intensive technical assets; and (3) eliminating performance reducing factors, for example an unsuitable system layout, process unbalance, or material flow disturbances.

A good example for modernization opportunities is the system IT. Hardware suppliers are dramatically increasing the support fees and spare parts prices for older systems. Even though software does not wear out, it has a limited life. After a period of usually five to seven years, most original suppliers stop supporting older operating system versions. Application software, for example data bases, also requires recent operating system versions. New software usually asks for new hardware and vice-versa. As a result, the end-users are forced to regularly update and upgrade their IT. For large systems, an IT upgrade is a quite complex task and needs a lot of preparation. Carrying out such projects requires an in-depth knowledge of the system and also access to interface specifications and to the source code of applications. Because IT usually is the most critical component in a system, there is no room for any mistakes. The system needs to be operational again at the planned time, and each day of delay means losing production. Therefore, the original suppliers have the best chances to win such orders.

Another good modernization opportunity are drives. As environmental aspects are increasingly important, power consumption becomes an issue. High efficiency electric motors have a significantly lower power consumption as compared to conventional ones. Generally, a positive business case for such a substitution can be assumed if the reduced long-term system operating costs not only overcompensate the initial investment into new equipment but also offset the waste of remaining life of the old components.

For customers, a special situation arises when systems are approaching their end of life. Especially if the long-term development of the business is not certain, the decision whether to invest in a new system or to continue running with the old one is often very difficult. In such a case, extending the life of the system and possibly also increasing its performance though upgrading and modernization could be the optimal solution.

Integrated service suppliers should actively pursue such modernization opportunities. They should develop attractive business cases and invite customers to joint workshops where such initiatives can be discussed. Demonstrating interest in keeping the systems updated and in improving their operational performance is also a proven way for ensuring high customer satisfaction.

A regular debate inside systems and installations companies is whether modernization projects should belong to the new systems or to the service business. An argument for allocating them to the new systems business is the project character of modernization works, which is comparable with the nature of system installation. On the other hand, modernization projects are usually significantly smaller and technically less complex.

An important reason for making modernization part of the service business is the fact that it always happens in the operations phase of systems, and therefore, these projects require a thorough coordination with the system operation. Systems may not be available the whole time, and modernization work could only be carried out during special windows allowed by operations. Modernization also needs close coordination with service activities. For each modernization step, service people have to make the system available and must put it back into operation when the works are finished.

Experience shows that installations companies that are allocating modernization to service manage to establish a stronger presence in the life cycle of their systems. One of the reasons is that if allocated to the new systems business, modernization is often treated like a stepchild. Systems people, technical as well as sales, usually regard modernization as less challenging and not really worth pursuing. They will rather concentrate on hunting for new systems, and modernization will always remain a second priority.

Modernization projects are a great opportunity for increasing the level of technological expertise of service organizations. With each new project, service people gain important new technical, technological, and project management competences. Being so close to the system, service technicians are in the best position for identifying modernization opportunities. Occasionally, they may be needing engineering support from the new systems group, but usually this could be scheduled accordingly. Certainly, if such projects exceed a certain technological complexity or size, they belong to the new systems business.

Typical modernization opportunities fitting well into service are: (1) projects with repetitive character. This means that once the solution has been developed, it can be rolled out on a larger scale. This is often the case with fleets or other large systems containing many similar parts; (2) projects not requiring substantial changes of the system layout and function, like when old or obsolete system components are replaced with new better ones.

5% Spare Parts Supply: Comprises all spare parts supply activities outside the O&M contracts.

As spare parts supply is generally integral part of O&M contracts, the stand-alone spare parts business usually does not have a large business share inside the portfolio of integrated service suppliers. Especially if the outsourcing maturity in the specific market segment is high, most spare parts are handled inside the service contracts. The relevance of the spare parts business (stand-alone or inside O&M) is also very dependent on the type of systems. Systems with many proprietary components that cannot be easily re-manufactured or substituted by other suppliers, critical systems, and systems with high safety requirements yield better opportunities for the spare parts business than systems with many standard components and simple mechanical or electrical parts. Some examples for areas where spare parts have high relevance are railway systems, power plants, and complex medical systems. All these areas are characterized by high technical complexity, high criticality, and high safety and security requirements. They also usually require suppliers with special authorizations. In these areas, the business share of spare parts supply can be significantly higher.

The spare parts business is often subject to false expectations. Smart customers always look at the openness of the systems they plan to purchase. They will usually prefer systems based on industry standards rather than ones with many proprietary components. They will also often require comprehensive spare parts lists with indication of the original manufacturers. Once the initial spare parts stock is used, whenever possible, customers will look for alternative sources for parts. They will seek for substitutes for all simple and uncritical items and will try to short-cut the system providers by directly contacting the original suppliers.

Regardless of the share of spare parts inside the business portfolio of service suppliers, an efficient spare parts organization and process are always a must. This is not only mandatory for ensuring high customer satisfaction but also indispensable for serving the own O&M projects.

Strategy and Tactics

The terms *Strategy* and *Tactics* are often used without further reflection. Few people can give them a proper definition and use them correctly.
A good explanation of these terms can be found in military theory. Carl von Clausewitz, the famous Prussian general and military theorist, defined them in the following manner:
Tactics is the study of the employment of fighting forces in battle. Strategy he describes as the study of the employment of battles for the object of the war.[1]

Transactional businesses, such as the systems and installations one, can make good use of terms and concepts anchored in military theory. In business, winning a war could mean conquering a desired market position or becoming the preferred supplier of an important customer, or it could simply mean knocking out a major competitor. For achieving their strategic goals, systems and installations companies have to win the projects (battles) defined in their business strategy. Without a smart strategy, the danger of wasting efforts in the wrong battles is great. For each contract opportunity that fits into the right direction, an individual tactical approach needs to be developed. Only a good tactical approach based on the customer's specific preferences, the own strengths, and on the weaknesses of the competitors will ensure the win.

---

[1] On War, Carl von Clausewitz, Berlin 1832

A consistent service strategy is made up of the following two elements:

The **Business Growth** strategy is aimed at the acquisition of new business. The **Business Protection** strategy must ensure that the own base of running contracts is protected and maintained.

These two main strategy elements determine all other supporting strategies, such as related to human resources, portfolio, and innovation.

Good strategic orientation does not only mean preparing a consistent strategy paper; it also means implementing it. Many companies spend a lot of effort on preparing strategies but fail in implementing them. Setting clear milestones in this regard and strictly controlling their fulfillment is an important management task.

Most service strategies are focusing too much on growth and fail in reflecting the fact that protecting the running business is at least as important. Without protecting, defending, and renewing contracts, service cannot grow. The systematic loss of running service contracts cannot be compensated by the acquisition of new ones. Military theory teaches that, in most cases, defense trumps attack. This is also true for the service business. The effort required for winning a new contract is much higher than the effort spent on protecting one. Therefore, business protection must be equally given much strategic attention. Successful service managers dedicate a significant amount of their efforts to their running contracts and to their current customers.

While business protection comprises many common elements, the business growth strategies differ substantially between integrated service suppliers and generic service providers.

Growth Strategy

For integrated service suppliers, the main source of growth are new service contracts following own new installations. A successful new systems business is a mandatory prerequisite for a growing service business. At the same time, it must be taken into consideration that only new systems projects with material service potential are relevant for the growth strategy of service. If the customer of a new installation follows a strict in-house service strategy, the potential for service is usually low and limited to just selling spare parts or offering on-call support. Therefore, the specific strategies of the systems and the service units must not only be individually consistent, but they should also support a common business goal. The overall strategies of systems and installations companies must clearly define the expected contribution of these two businesses to the overall result, the rules of cooperation, and the selection criteria for new projects. The main strategic focus of service regarding the business growth must be set on maximizing the capitalization on the opportunities yielded by the installation of own new systems. Thus, it must be aiming at the services with the broadest scope and highest business impact. This is the integral operation and maintenance (O&M) of large systems and installations. Some systems and installations companies shy away from tackling these opportunities because they fear the risks related to taking over the global technical responsibility for a large system in operation. They also fear the personnel risk related to the high number of headcounts generally required in large O&M projects. Instead, they prefer to sell just support services, like hot-line, planned maintenance, and spare parts

supply, usually linked to their proprietary systems and components. Even though these services generate relatively high profits, they are not sufficient for sustaining an ambitious service growth strategy.
Successful integrated service suppliers always try to take over the integral maintenance and technical operation for their new systems. While maintenance is a relatively common portfolio element, technical operation services, for example ***control room**** and ***field operations****, usually do not receive enough attention. Some of these activities can be combined with maintenance ones, thus allowing a higher utilization of service personnel. Especially during the starting phase, the customers' personnel may be overstrained by the complexity of tasks linked to the operation of new large systems. The risk of losing production, of damaging the system due to handling errors, or of not being able to deal with emergency situations is quite high when new large installations go live. Suppliers should bring this risk into the attention of their customers and actively offer to take over the entire technical operation of the system or propose to set up a mixed operations team.

As also described later in more detail, competition has a different relevance in the service for new systems than in the service for existing ones. For the installation of new systems, competition might be fierce, but once this order has been awarded, the integrated service supplier has the best chances for winning the new service contract. In only exceptional cases, for example if the supplier renders a poor installation job, external competition could be of relevance. Therefore, integrated service suppliers should concentrate on supporting the win of new systems by developing a consistent system life cycle approach and by convincing the customer that, with them, his system will be in best hands.

Over the entire life of a system, service costs can sum up to significant amounts, sometimes in the magnitude of the initial system investment. Today, when customers plan to buy a new system, they increasingly shift their focus on the Total Cost of Ownership (TCO) and ask for offers comprising the system as well as the long-term service. Thus, beside an attractive system price, lowest possible service costs are also of great importance. For service, supporting the win of new systems means to actively participate in the development of attractive life-cycle solutions. Together with the systems colleagues, service people need to develop comprehensive TCO models for their installations. Such models should not only focus on the initial investment and direct service costs but should also address obsolescence issues and long-term upgrading and modernization requirements. The focus on TCO sometimes puts service in a difficult situation. In tight negotiations, some suppliers are willing to sacrifice the service for the purpose of increasing their chances for winning the system order. This often pushes service in the role of the spoilsport. After the discussions regarding the system part are concluded, everybody is looking at and expects service to provide the final argument for the contract award. A too aggressive service approach may backfire years later, and by that time nobody will remember the circumstances under which the service offer was made. Therefore, service managers should define their threshold regarding the lowest acceptable service price. For large contacts, going beyond should only happen with the clear endorsement of the company's CEO and should be documented and reflected accordingly in the service targets and the business planning.

Even though in most cases the system offer has the highest relevance, under life-cycle considerations, a competitive and consistent service offer is of great importance for winning an installations contract. A technically consistent and economically attractive service offering is always also a good indication for the quality of the system. Knowing that later on the chances for changing horses are rather low, mature customers will put a lot of emphasis on the maturity of their future service provider. Therefore, demonstrating the own service capabilities as soon in the bidding process as possible, for example by organizing visits to reference service sites, can have a major positive impact.

For integrated service suppliers, defining the growth strategy is quite straight forward. With regard to regions and customers, service simply follows the own installations. Insofar, the 'battles' are clear and tactical aspects come into the focus.

Ramping up a large service organization for a new project is a complex job and needs a lot of preparation. In some regions, good service people are hard to find in the local labor market and must be brought over from other regions. For strategic reasons or taxation purposes, in some projects, it may be required to set up a new service company. In some countries, this is not straight forward and may require partnering with a local company. All these boundary conditions need to be taken into consideration already during the offering phase of a new system.

If service is awarded together with the system, the time needed for the installation is usually long enough to allow a proper preparation of the service project. Such a parallel system-service award is the exception though. Most customers insist on receiving a binding service offer from the supplier right from the very beginning but prefer to decide about the service award in the later phases of the system installation. Their intention is to have an additional lever on the supplier which they potentially could use for forcing him to accept certain compromises or just to give away some 'goodies'. "I'll give you also the service if you..." is something suppliers often hear from their customers. With a binding service offer already in their hands, customers could also use the time to double-check their own service strategy with regard to outsourcing. Sometimes, they award the service very late and thus put their suppliers under great time pressure.

For large service projects, the tactical approach must be elaborated before the offer preparation starts. Such tactic must comprise all relevant factors considered decisive for winning the contract, including customer preferences, differentiation from competition, and unique selling points. Depending of the system criticality, the operating requirements, and the end-user's life-cycle strategy, the service offer must be specifically developed and should accentuate the aspects of most importance for the customer. Most requests for proposal (RFP) are not specific enough in this regard, and suppliers should not shy away from asking the customers about their preferences and priorities. The tactical approach should also comprise all preparation activities required for ramping up the new service organization in the shortest possible time and at lowest possible costs. It must define the optimal project set-up, possibly as a combination of own resources and sub-suppliers. Recruiting and training of personnel resources are of great importance. Even though some people can be taken over from the installation team, the majority of service people need to be hired from scratch. It must be determined where these people should come from and which activities are required as a preparation. A particular aspect that needs consideration is the general reluctance of installation people to work in service projects. 24/7 shift work scares off many people. Furthermore, because service has a direct impact on the operation, and thus on the customer's business, the work pressure in service is usually higher than during installation. Trouble with the system always exposes service technicians to high stress. Pressure also arises from the daily interaction with the customers' operational people, who are not always friendly. Motivating technicians to move from installation to service often requires increasing their pay. Because service for large installations is a local people's business, good understanding of the local labor market conditions and labor law is mandatory.

Sometimes, customers prefer to execute the service for their systems with own resources. This could be the case for several reasons. Some customers may fear the loss of control over the service activities. Others may need to ensure the jobs of their own employees or may have concerns regarding the confidentiality and security of their information. In many situations when customers do not want to outsource services, suppliers give up to easily. There are a couple of interesting alternatives which still could make a substantial participation of the supplier in the execution of services possible.

If the customer's concerns are about securing the jobs of own employees, taking over a certain number of these people could be a good solution. Such a personnel transfer is generally perceived by the suppliers as well as by the customers as too complicated, and therefore such a solution is often not taken into consideration. With a proper clarification regarding the handling of personnel issues at contract termination, most concerns on both sides could be eliminated. All other matters, such as employment conditions and pensions, can be solved if the partners are genuinely interested in cooperating and in finding a solution.

Setting up a joint service company is another very interesting alternative. In this scenario, customers and suppliers establish a joint company with the business purpose of servicing the customer's system. The company is controlled by an advisory board made up of representatives of both parties. It receives its own business targets from the board and is supposed to generate profit. This profit is then shared between the customer and the supplier according to their participation in the joint company. The company should work on a cost-plus basis. The payment received from the customer should reimburse for all company's direct and indirect costs and also include a variable incentive-based profit. The board defines the annual cost budget and the incentive mechanism. The incentive scheme should be annually adapted on a consensual basis to reflect the concrete needs of the customer's business. For avoiding that one party optimizes itself at the cost of the other, the parties may also agree on a minimum and a maximum profit level. Joint service companies solve many problems which cannot be properly addressed in most other service models. Customers still retain a fair share of control over the service for their systems. The joint company is fully transparent to both parties. Each partner can transfer people into it as needed for establishing the best possible set-up. For example, customers could provide technology specialists who know the process, while suppliers could contribute with experts in the latest service methods and tools.

While offering the service for own installations is a must for integrated service suppliers, service for third-party systems should be acquired only on a selective basis. The growth strategy should define the extent of such endeavors, for example as a certain share of the total business or by setting clear eligibility criteria for such projects. Generally, only projects of strategic relevance should be tackled, like in the case of strongly growing markets or customers with interesting development plans.

As already addressed, upgrading, modernization, and system improvement are business elements that could fall into the responsibility of the system units but would potentially also fit well into the portfolio of service. If they are allocated to service, the growth strategy must clearly address also these opportunities. Service suppliers should develop and constantly adapt their portfolio in this regard, by focusing on solutions of high (and measurable!) customer value and preferably of repetitive nature.

The chances of generic providers to win the service for new systems are rather low. Therefore, their main growth path is to push competitors out of their running contracts. To be successful requires selecting the targets with the highest chances, such as those contracts where customers are dissatisfied with the services they receive from their current supplier. This kind of business (brown-field) does not ask for a sophisticated personnel strategy, as most of the required people can be taken over from the incumbent suppliers. Price is always the prevailing winning argument, and often the only one. Because customers usually expect a reduction of the service price with each new contract term, suppliers are always under great pressure. As a result, the service quality decreases over time, and thus the technical condition of the systems continuously degrades. The actual technical system condition is an important parameter that needs consideration during offer preparation. Though, it is often ignored and is backfiring later during project execution.

Business growth can also be achieved through acquisitions. At first sight, such a strategy may seem attractive, but it only rarely leads to sustainable long-term results. An acquisition only makes sense if it has strategic or technological relevance. A strategic reason could be, for example, the access to an important new customer or market. From a technological perspective, the gain of important subject matter expertise or the portfolio enlargement with additional products and services could be good reasons for buying a business. Acquiring a service company just for boosting business figures usually does not make sense. The value of such companies lies mainly in the value of their contracts. Generic service contracts are always subject to intense competition, and the risk of losing them after expiration is high. So, why pay for such contracts if one could get them for free a couple of years later when they are out again on the market.

Because of the complexity of O&M projects for large installations, addressing all potential business opportunities is not possible. Jumping from one opportunity to the next without a proper selection increases the risk of bad projects and poor financial results. This is especially important with regard to running service contracts of other suppliers which are due for renewal. Not every opportunity is a good one. Customers who frequently change their service suppliers are often difficult to please and are not interested in establishing a strong supplier relationship. Successful companies develop long-term business strategies focusing on the most promising opportunities.

Protection Strategy

Service is a cumulative business. Because service projects have a duration of several years, they generate revenues and profits over a longer period of time. Thus, over time, new projects are adding to running ones, building a solid contract base which needs to be protected. This is equally relevant for integrated service suppliers as well as for generic service providers.

For integrated service suppliers, a critical situation may arise when new service contracts come closer to their first expiration date. This is the time when customers may start thinking about opening competition. Usually reluctant to really change their supplier, they often re-tender a contract with the main objective of putting the incumbent under pressure. Nevertheless, this could be the opportunity competition was waiting for. Competitors may think that once all infant system deficiencies have been eliminated the installation can be expected to run free of trouble over the next period. In this regard, the biggest threat for integrated service suppliers are generic service providers. Because they do not have an own systems business, snatching contracts from others is their main business model. If they see a chance to throw competitors out of their contracts, they will take it. Therefore, integrated service providers should start early (at least one year before contract expiration) preparing for this critical moment. If they succeed in renewing their contract for additional terms, competitors will increasingly be discouraged and will lose their interest.

If the contract conditions are favorable and long-term contractual risks are not anticipated, including prolongation options into their contracts is something service providers (and also customers) should always consider. Especially if service contracts are subject to public procurement law, extension options can be of great advantage for both parties. If the customer is satisfied with the services he has been receiving during the regular contract period, he could extend the contract for another couple of years and thus save the effort required for preparing a new tender. Even if the contract does not contain such options and public procurement law requires a new tender, there are situations in which customers could still extend the contract beyond its original duration. Such reasons could be, for instance, pending works which only the service incumbent can execute or time constraints in the preparation of the new tender as a result from a special business situation.

Customer satisfaction is always of great importance. It often happens that after a while customers take excellent service for granted and forget how 'happy' they are. They may start thinking about why paying a lot of money if the system runs smoothly. Suppliers should not allow such a loss of awareness to happen, especially in the final contract phase. Towards the end of a contract, they must intensify the dialogue with their customer and should not forget to emphasize the value contribution of their services to his business success.

Suppliers should prepare their tactic regarding the renewal of expiring contracts carefully and in due time. Such tactic should comprise all required activities regarding the customer, the competitors, and the own organization, as well as the timing of these actions. During this phase, suppliers need to also be aware of possible raiding attempts of competitors hunting for key personnel they would need for taking over the contract. Waiting until the very last moment before addressing the customers regarding a near contract expiration is sometimes a good tactic. The lack of time for preparing a solid tender could determine them to pull an extension option if such an option is existent or to prolong the contract for some time.
With enough time on their side, customers may start thinking about how they could optimize the contract for themselves, for example by dividing it into proprietary and commodity packages, with the intent of finding a cheap supplier for the latter. If

such a scenario is deemed possible, suppliers should engage early into discussions with their customers to prevent a loss of control over the situation.

Service suppliers should never give customers the impression of fearing competition. This applies not only for the protection of running contracts but also for the acquisition of new ones. Customers may interpret such fear as an indication that competition might be capable of offering something better than their current supplier. Contract incumbents cannot prevent that competitors may contact their customer. Especially strategic customers, such as ones with large expansion plans, are always in the focus of competition. In many cases, competitors have to deal with the challenge of not having a real relationship with the customer yet. Therefore, they will do everything to establish a bridgehead inside the customer's business. A typical opportunity for gaining such access are small auxiliary projects the customer may be planning to execute. In such a situation, competitors may step in with extremely low prices just to get the job. If they succeed, they will use this opportunity for convincing the customer that they are generally more efficient and capable of offering better value for money. They will usually pretend to have a competitive edge resulting from more advanced service methods and innovation; which also helps them in justifying the low price of their offer. As a result, customers may start thinking about trying out new ways also for their main contracts. Any service contract, even a small one, is a good vehicle for establishing an ongoing customer relationship which can be gradually developed. The potential loss of money on a particular small job is a price most competitors are happily willing to pay for finding a path into the organization of a new customer.

Suppliers should never make the mistake to think of being on the safe side forever and that getting all their customers' new jobs will automatically happen. Customer organizations are often non-homogeneous, with different parties rivaling on different matters. The service strategy is a common subject of dissent inside the customers' organizations. Some people may think the current supplier is perfect, while others are of the opinion that trying out a new one would be a good idea. Therefore, suppliers should always be alert, stay in control, and be prepared to defend the attacks from competition.

Systems and installations companies must define a consistent global strategy including new systems and service. Usually, global company strategies put a lot of emphasis on the systems business and say very little about service. It is quite uncommon that systems and installations companies select their targets for the acquisition of new systems contracts also on the basis of their service potential, for instance by prioritizing those opportunities where customers are likely to outsource services. In most company strategies, the role of service is not clear. Should service just support the systems business, or should it be regarded as a second business pillar equally relevant as the systems one? Even though declaring service as a first-tier business, many systems and installations companies fail in establishing appropriate boundary conditions to allow service developing to its best. For example, poor standardization in the area of systems and components is a big obstacle for efficient service. If IT solutions differ significantly from one installation to another, it is impossible for service to maintain a sufficient number of specialists for supporting all installed systems throughout their life cycle. If the variety of components, e.g.

motors, used in a system is too large, keeping enough spare parts in stock becomes very expensive. Poor system documentation also puts service in great difficulty, for instance if the version of a specific item cannot be identified.

Defining a precise mission statement for service is important. Such statement must clearly specify the sources of service growth. Shall service concentrate just on own systems or also on third-party installations? And to which extent? Is the profit dilution generally inherent to the acquisition of service for third-party systems acceptable? The service portfolio must also be accurately defined. A clear allocation of system upgrades and modernization to either service or to the systems units is often missing, usually leading to internal friction and disputes regarding business mandates.

Planning

The systems and installations business is usually composed of two parts: one related to the installation of new systems and the other in charge of servicing and sometimes also of technically operating the installed base of own systems. Generally, the service business is less volatile than the systems one and therefore easier to plan. This specificity will be explained later in more detail. For many systems and installations companies, service is an important business stabilization factor helping them to overcome periods of low investment into new systems.

The correct planning of service requires considering a couple of special aspects of this type of business. Even though most of these aspects are rather obvious, many managers, and especially those with other prior professional backgrounds, either do not know them or fail, sometimes even refuse, to consider them in their business planning. This often leads to false expectations, erroneous business targets and plans, and also to frustration among service people.

A couple of false paradigms regarding the service business continue to persist in the minds of many managers.

1. Service business is per se (by itself) a high profit business.

Clarifying this statement requires defining first what can be considered a high and what a low profit business. For the service of large installations, a double-digit profitability (EBIT) can be considered as high. In the spare parts business and on-call service, the profitability can be higher. Service profits will be generally higher, the more sophisticated and proprietary the systems are. Servicing such complex systems requires in-depth technological expertise which, in most cases, in-house service organizations of customers and generic service providers cannot acquire. Frequent reasons are the inaccessibility of the required knowledge or the fact that keeping such highly skilled service personnel in the own organization might not be economically feasible. Some business areas are very sensitive with regard to the operational safety of systems; therefore, the service for these systems is highly regulated. Servicing such systems often requires compliance with high quality standards and special authorizations. In all these cases, competition from other service providers and in-house service organizations is lower, thus higher profits are possible.

At the other end, broad base services like maintaining and technically operating industrial installations of lower complexity are under strong competitive pressure from generic service providers and from in-house service organizations. This kind of service usually requires engaging large numbers of low to medium skilled service personnel executing repetitive and rather simple mechanical and electrical maintenance tasks. As the numbers and qualifications of service people as well as the local labor rates are no secret, this business is generally quite transparent. Sometimes, the numbers and qualifications of service personnel are even dictated by the customers in their requests for proposal. Thus, customers can determine with some approximation the cost structure of a service project. On top of this cost estimation, they will only accept a small mark-up for functional costs and a rather moderate profit, usually in the low to medium single digit range. Another aspect of relevance for the profitability of service is the price erosion caused by immature competitors. These suppliers, in most cases generic and local players, are often trying to win contracts by offering very low prices which no solid provider could match. Even though most customers, often as a result of own bad experiences with poor service quality in the past, do not seriously consider such providers, they will still use their offers as a price benchmark to put pressure on the suppliers they really prefer.

There are many different types of service. Each of them is characterized by its own particularities, requires its individual skill set and organizational set-up, and yields its specific range of profits. Assuming that any of these aspects can be simply extrapolated form on type of service to another would be a mistake. Unfortunately, many managers still step into this pitfall. This happens especially often when managers with other prior professional backgrounds, such as products and systems, start into the managing of a service business for large installations.

2. *Service business must always be significantly more profitable than the installations business.*

Assuming this on a general basis is incorrect. In some areas of activity, this could be true as the result of a special business policy of system providers called 'razor blade' approach. The system, in analogy to the razor, is offered at very competitive prices, while service takes the role of the expensive razor blade. In the business for large installations, this policy is not applicable. One of the reasons is that, most times, the system and the pertaining longer-term service are negotiated and awarded in one package with a strong focus of customers on TCO. Thus, service offers must be very competitive to not endanger the whole deal. Another reason for rather moderate service profits is, as mentioned earlier, the relatively high transparency of costs.

For commodity installations of small to medium size, low complexity, and low degree of automation, the achievable profits for the system and for the pertaining comprehensive service are comparable and usually in a low to medium single digit range.

In larger installations with high complexity and a significant share of proprietary systems, like automation, IT, and sophisticated electro-mechanical components, service profits can be a couple of percentage points higher than in the systems business. For such systems, customers are accepting a 'complexity premium' and are prepared to pay a higher price because they fear the risk exposure related to poor service. Additionally, they usually prefer to engage the original supplier for the service of their equipment, at least for the first couple of years.

A frequent reason why in practice the profit quality in the systems business is sometimes significantly lower than in service is the profit dilution caused by installation projects performing below expectations. This is a common phenomenon that can be observed for most systems and installations companies. While planning errors or technical deficiencies always have a direct and immediate negative impact on installation projects, problems in service projects can usually be sorted out over the duration of longer-term contracts. Experience shows that even service contracts with a problematic start can be developed to generate an acceptable level of profit over their entire duration, provided that they are properly managed. A frequent planning mistake made by systems and installations companies is the attempt to compensate profits below expectations in the installations business by increasing the profit expectations for service. Apart from leading to exaggerated and unrealistic service targets, this bad habit deflects the attention from fixing the root causes of problems in the installation projects.

Stepping away from these erroneous paradigms and professionally assessing the business on the basis of proven facts will lead to significantly more solid and sustainable business plans.

Market Assessment

Generally, the service market is made up of four main segments. From an integrated service supplier's perspective, the relevance of these markets is as follows:

- Services for the installed base of own systems (***brown-field service****)
  This is the largest and most important market for all mature integrated service suppliers. Successful companies should retain at least 80% of the accessible market share. Part of this market may be occupied by in-house service departments of customers, and therefore captive (not accessible). Service for smaller systems of less complexity may be acquired by other generic service providers. This contract base needs to be maintained and protected against the attacks of competition, especially when running service contracts are expiring and must be renewed. This market should be in the main focus of any integrated service supplier's protection strategy.

- Services for own new systems going into operation (***green-field service****)
  This is the most relevant market with regard to business growth and should be the first priority in the growth strategy of integrated service suppliers. A certain share

of this market may be inaccessible because some customers may decide to execute the technical services for their new systems in-house. Successful companies usually acquire at least 90% of the accessible market. Keeping competitors out of this market is especially important. Losing the initial service contract for a large system to another party (other than the customer's own in-house service department) would result in a significant loss of reputation. It is also important to keep in mind that the window of opportunity for service usually closes forever once the first service term is lost. The entry barriers for regaining such contracts are high.

- Services for the installed system base of other suppliers (brown-field service)
  For generic service providers, who do not have an own systems business, this is the main market segment. Their business model consists in taking over contracts from other competitors.
  For integrated service suppliers, this market is of low relevance. For the service of large and complex third-party systems, the entry barriers are high. The original supplier may already be rendering the services for many years. In many other cases, the services are executed by generic service providers or by the customers' in-house service departments. In all these situations, customers are rather reluctant to change horses, especially if they are satisfied with the performance of their current providers.

- Services for new systems installed by other suppliers (green field service)
  This market segment is also of low relevance. For the

> service of large and complex systems the entry barriers are high because of the risks stemming from proprietary systems and components, for example IT and automation. Therefore, most of this market is occupied by the original suppliers or by the customers' in-house service departments; thus, it is captive.

Assessing the market potential for the installation of new systems is straight forward. The sum of all new installations planned by the customers in a specific year determines the market size. A common mistake is made by linking the size and development of the service market to the size and development of the new systems one. The service market is mainly determined by the total installed systems base of previous years and is made up just to a small extent by service opportunities generated through the installation of new systems. In mature markets, the installed systems base is significantly larger than the incremental annual increase stemming from new systems. This can be easily proven by the following very simplified model. For example, under the theoretical assumption that the cargo market would be stagnating (which means that the cargo tonnage remains at the same level over a longer period of time), new cargo systems would only have to replace systems reaching their end of life. Further assuming that the average life span of cargo systems is 20 years, the amount of systems needing to be substituted in one particular year would equal to 1/20 of the total installed base. Thus, the installed base would be approximately 19 times larger than the base of new systems installed in that particular year. Regarding the service market dynamics, the high weight of the installed base has the role of a strong attenuation factor. Due to the fact that in mature markets the installed base is much larger than the size of the annual new installations (the main source of service growth), the service market is significantly less volatile than the new systems one. For the same reason, the growth rate of the service market is rather low. During periods with strong investments into new assets, the relative (in %) service market growth will be substantially lower than the relative growth of the new systems one. On the other hand, during low investment periods, when the new systems market shrinks, the service market would theoretically still grow.

A further aspect that needs consideration in the assessment of the service market is the fact that service opportunities triggered by new installations usually materialize with a delay of two to three years required for building the system and for putting it into operation.

The accurate translation of the systems base (installed systems as well as new ones) into service potential is a challenging task and requires taking into account many different aspects including:

- Outsourcing maturity in the respective market
- Type of targeted service, for example O&M, technical operation, planned maintenance, spare parts supply, or on-call service
- System age and technical condition
- System complexity and degree of automation
- Local labor rates

Some indicators, like the ***maintenance factor****[*] of equipment, help to roughly determine the service potential of systems. The maintenance factor is defined as the total annual maintenance costs divided by the asset replacement value (ARV) of a system. It can be applied for new systems as well as for installed ones.

For larger and more complex industrial installations, this indicator is in the range of 2% to 4% and varies with the system type, its age, its utilization, and with the cost of labor. More details can be found in technical literature. For example, an installation with an asset replacement value of 100 mil Euros and a maintenance factor of 3% would require total annual maintenance costs of 3 mil Euros. Additionally to maintenance, the market for technical operation should also be taken into consideration.

New Orders and Sales

Successful service organizations generate the majority of their new orders by renewing their running contracts. Larger service contracts usually have a duration of three to five years. If the provider has rendered a good service during the running contract period, his chances for renewing the contract are rather high, usually between 70 and 90%. Renewing a running contract is generally far easier to than acquiring a new one. One reason are the relatively high mobilization efforts and costs which any competitor needs to consider in his offer and which the contract incumbent can save. Another reason is the general reluctance of customers to expose themselves to the operational risk associated with a change of the service provider. Therefore, maintaining the base of running contracts must always be of highest priority for any service provider.

It is very important to understand that the base of running contracts is always subject to a certain erosion related to various aspects like the potential loss of contracts, reductions in service scope due to the insourcing of activities, and price reductions required by customers. It is often the case that towards the end of the first contract period, customers want to take over certain works, typically commodity mechanical or electrical tasks, to save costs. This can also happen later with any further contract extension. Latest with the first contract renewal, customers are also expecting suppliers to share productivity gains and thus reduce the service price. Experience shows that even a solid provider with excellent customer satisfaction scores and high contract retention rates should consider an erosion of his running contract base of yearly 3% to 5%. From a total revenue perspective, this erosion could be partially compensated by inflation, which is mainly determined by the increase of labor rates.

Therefore, acquiring new business in order to maintain and preferably expand the contract base is a must.
For integrated service suppliers, gaining the majority of the new service contract opportunities stemming from own new installations is a mission-critical goal. This is especially important for large and complex systems with high service potential. If the customers do not have the intention to maintain the new systems with own resources, the chances for the integrated service suppliers of receiving the service contracts are high, usually above 90%. At least for the initial term of such service contracts, the integrated service suppliers have a significant advantage against competition. They can start setting up the future service organization already during the installation and commissioning of the new system. Actively engaging service people already in this early project phase is a very cost-efficient method which saves mobilization costs and time. Furthermore, some of the technicians engaged in the system installation can be taken over into the service project. This way it can be ensured that when the system goes into operation, a sufficient number of well-qualified people are available for starting the service project.

If customers favor an in-house solution, integrated service suppliers should always try to point out how a win-win situation could still be established through smart service partnership models. This aspect was already addressed in the *Strategy* chapter.

For third-party service suppliers, it is usually quite hard to deal with the complexity of larger systems and with proprietary system components, and therefore their chances of winning such contracts are low.

As already mentioned, special attention during planning must be also given to opportunities for offering additional technical operation services, such as control room and field operations.

Furthermore, additional business opportunities like enlarging the base of serviced equipment and offering system overhauls and modernization must also not be neglected.

In the business mix of integrated service suppliers, services for the own installed base represent the by far largest component with a share of usually 80% to 90%. With this strong focus on own systems, the main source of service growth are own new installations going live. Thus, service growth is closely linked to a solid and consistent new systems business. Even though this aspect is obvious, it is often forgotten or sometimes even voluntarily ignored when service business targets are set. Too often, and especially when the systems and installations business is performing below expectations, service is blindly declared the #1 element of the company's growth strategy. Because of the cumulative nature of service contracts, service business will normally always grow; however, the growth rate is mainly determined by the success of the new systems and installations business. Without new systems, the pipeline for new service orders dries out, and thus service cannot grow.

Integrated service suppliers should offer services for third-party systems only on a selective basis. For large systems, the entry barriers for service are quite high. Complexity, proprietary components, and unknown technical system condition are some of the factors speaking against such an undertaking. For systems of low or medium complexity, competition from small local companies is very intense. Service opportunities for third-party systems should be carefully evaluated from a strategic perspective. Answering questions like "Is this customer going to expand his system in near future, or is he planning the installation of new systems?" help in selecting the right targets. Already being a customer's service provider often represents a decisive advantage in the acquisition of new installation business.

Accounting principles usually require booking the order intake for multi-year contracts in one piece at the time when the order is received. Generally, most long-term service contracts are handled this way. Booking the order in yearly slices would only be allowed if the contract could be prematurely terminated by the customer and if the likelihood for such a termination is high. This could be, for example, the case if the customer is allowed to terminate the contract for convenience and if there are good reasons that he will do so before the end of the regular term. The same applies to contracts containing very demanding performance requirements, where not achieving these targets may result in a breach and consequentially in a termination. In conclusion, the order intake may significantly vary over the years depending on the booking of multi-year service contracts. Expecting the service order intake to always grow from one year to the next is a common planning mistake in this regard.

Constant growth could be expected in the case of some more linear service areas like the spare parts supply; but it is never the case if large long-term service contracts prevail, such as in the O&M business. For reporting purposes, the one-time booking of multi-year contracts is often mandatory. For business analysis purposes, the order intake needs to be evaluated on a normalized basis. This means that for each year only the respective yearly slice of multi-year contracts should be considered.

If service is awarded together with the system, there could be a significant delay between the order intake and the recognition of the respective revenues. This delay is determined by the time required for building the system and for putting it into operation. In many such cases, the service order will be subject to substantial changes because of variations of the system during the installation phase. Service providers need to carefully observe such variations and adapt their service offers accordingly.

Service revenues are easier to plan because they usually follow a regular pattern. This is especially the case of smaller contracts where the Completed Contract (CC) accounting method applies. According to this method, the whole contract is split in equal slices and revenue recognition occurs on a monthly base. For larger contracts, usually the Percentage of Completion (PoC) method, which recognizes sales in parallel to the progression of costs, is applied. As in large O&M contracts most of the expenses are personnel related and the personnel structure is usually rather stable, the progression of costs is also quite linear. Therefore, the planning of revenues is generally straight forward for the majority of service transactions. For modernization projects, the progression of costs is usually uneven, and planning requires a more detailed effort.

Steadily growing revenues are a good indicator for a growing business. At least in short term. Assessing the mid and long-term sustainability of service requires looking at additional parameters. A strong backlog is always a valuable asset and an indication for a solid business. An annual book-to-bill ratio (orders divided by revenues) of greater than 1 is also generally considered an indication for a growing business. In service though, the book-to-bill ratio could be misleading because of the special nature of multi-year service contracts. It will be higher in years when long-term contracts are booked and lower in years when such bookings are missing. Thus, in the service business for large installations the book-to-bill ratio should be interpreted yearly on the basis of its rolling average over a longer period of time. For example, this indicator could be determined by averaging the result of the previous year with the forecast for the current year and with the planning values for the future two to three years. The total time span for the rolling book-to-bill calculation should be individually defined for each business based on the average duration of large service contracts. Such an averaged value of greater than 1 would be a reliable indication for a healthy and growing service business. Furthermore, the series made up by the yearly values calculated as described above would provide a more reliable information about the long them development and sustainability of the business.

Business targets usually include new orders as one of the most important parameters. This strong focus on orders sometimes leads to a lot of irritation, especially towards the end of the business year. The date for receiving a large order can never be precisely predicted. Negotiations are complex and extensive, and many unforeseen events can pop up, such as delays in the system installation or new decision makers on the customer side. If the award of an important order is getting delayed and potentially could be slipping over the edge of the fiscal year, people often get very nervous and emotional. If the order is received in the last day of the year, everything is fine. If it comes in one day later, it suddenly loses its relevance, and the responsible manager is blamed. For the business itself, such a delay of course has absolutely no significance. Still, the manager's incentives would be negatively affected, and the order would be put on top of his next year's targets. The frustration caused by such practice can be easily imagined. Sometimes, this order intake hysteria towards the year's end takes bizarre forms. It happens that concessions (price reductions, additional services) are made just for persuading the customers to sign the order faster. It is in the interest of their business that systems and installations companies define a smart policy regarding the planning of orders. A possible approach would be to generally plan orders which are expected towards the end of the fiscal year for the beginning of the next one. Instead of focusing on a strong 4th quarter, which is what most companies do, smart managers should rather focus on a strong 1st quarter.

Profit and Risk–Opportunity Management

Service profit generally follows the progression of revenues and costs. Therefore, its planning may appear simple. What makes it difficult though is the fact that it requires a good understanding of the risks and the opportunities related to large service contracts.

In the O&M business, some critical risks cannot be directly controlled by the service provider. Most O&M contracts have performance clauses regarding the fulfillment of certain performance levels the system is expected to achieve during operation. Even though the conformance with these requirements needs to be demonstrated during system acceptance, such trials never reflect the real conditions during live system operation. It could still be the case that design errors, unproven solutions, or unreliable components cause trouble even after the system has passed the final acceptance. Therefore, the potential risk that the system could fail yielding the contractual performance is still present. Usually, the integrated service supplier has to bear the negative consequences. These could take the form of liquidated damages for missed performance or of an increased maintenance effort and thus higher service costs. By the time these deficiencies become visible, the systems departments may already be engaged in new projects, with only limited resources and motivation to attend the proper remedy of the installation. Service managers need to be aware of these challenges. For systems and installations companies, the problem remains in the house, and customers do not really care which department of the supplier is responsible if the system fails in achieving the promised performance. Service managers must insist on a clear internal regulation with the systems departments regarding the policy for addressing such problems. Additionally, this risk can also be mitigated by including certain contingency clauses into the service contracts regarding the system performance. These aspects will be addressed in more detail later in the *Contracts* chapter.

Even though the system may have the intrinsic operating capabilities as contractually required and even though all services are carried out thoroughly, the system still could fail. This happens, for example, when IT or control systems crash, and, as a consequence, the whole system goes down. In this case, the operation may be stopped for several hours or even days, and the customer may incur high damages because of lost production. In many O&M contracts, liability for such damages is not excluded, and the service provider may be forced to compensate the customer for incurred losses. Depending on the criticality of the system, such damages can easily sum up to a couple of hundred thousand or even millions of Euros. This potential menace scares many suppliers. Though, in practice such (direct and consequential) damages are seldom applied. As it will be explained later in the *Supplier's Liability* section in more detail, suppliers should not be too afraid of this threat. At this point, is important to understand that the risk related to these damages cannot be absorbed inside the project. Damages summing up to a couple of hundred thousand Euros would drive any O&M project into deep losses and cannot be compensated by the reversal of risk accruals accumulated in that project. Therefore, any engagement into contracts entailing risks related to such damages should be assessed by also taking into account the general resilience of the entire business.

The likelihood of occasionally having to pay liquidated damages can be higher. Usually, such liquidated damages range in between 5% to 20% of the monthly payment and are also usually capped in aggregate for the entire contract. Therefore, risk contingencies have to be included into the contract calculation, and risk accruals need to be built accordingly during contract execution. Usually, the risk contingency for contractual risks ranges in between 1% to 3% of the total contract value, depending on the contract terms. A common mistake is made by releasing risk contingencies to early. This may positively influence the profit in one particular year, but it may lead to a risk under-coverage for the rest of the contract duration. For complex systems, failures are usually hard to predict and cannot be ruled out. Thus, the risk exposure remains until the very last day of the contract. A good practice would be to build related risk accruals over the first half of a contract and to gradually release them in the second one.

Personnel related risks also need attention, especially if changes in the local labor market can be expected. This would be, for instance, the case if larger development projects (infrastructure, construction) are planned in the respective region. Such projects would immediately drain the local market of its labor resources, and consequentially labor costs and personnel fluctuation would increase. Over the entire duration of a service project, such developments are not easy to anticipate. For longer term contracts (five and more years) the development of labor costs is an elusive factor and usually hard to predict. Thus, this risk needs to be properly reflected in the risk scheme of every long-term project and managed accordingly. It is highly recommended to introduce contract clauses by which suppliers and customers share this risk fairly. More details in this regard will be provided in the *Contracts* chapter.

Some technical risks such as the underestimation of required manpower, the over-consumption of spare parts, or excessive repairs are rather straightforward to deal with. If they lose their substantiation, for instance if the system does not require more spare parts than planned, the associated risk accruals can be released earlier.

Systematically pursuing profit improvement opportunities is as important as managing risk. The most relevant opportunities are related to productivity gains. Once the service project organization wears in, work can be planned and executed more efficiently. People get increasingly acquainted with the system and can enhance their skills level by training on the job. In the service for large installations, where up to 90% of the costs are personnel related, productivity improvement mainly means completing the required tasks with less people. Additional savings can be achieved by reducing the spare parts consumption, by systematically eliminating activities with no proven value, by eliminating recurrent failures, and by optimizing the engagement of subcontractors.

Experience shows that in well-calculated large service contracts and under the premises that the systems perform as planned and the contract is managed properly mature service providers can achieve up to 4% of savings in the second year, up to 2% in the third, and 0.5% in each of the following two years (always compared to the previous year). After that, further efficiency gains will be harder to achieve. Latest with the start of the second contract term, customers will usually ask for price reductions by pointing on potential productivity gains they expect their contractors of having achieved.

Sales

On-call support and spare parts supply are services which the system end-users need anyway for backing up their own service organizations. Selling these services is quite straight forward and mostly just a matter of performance level and price. From a customer's perspective, these services are a purely operational matter; thus, the buying decision is usually made by the in-house service managers.

The outsourcing of the integral service for a complete system is a matter of strategic relevance. Therefore, selling such services is much more complex. The buying decision is usually made at the top level of the company. The outsourcing maturity of companies varies a lot across the different business sectors. Generally, the more technical a customer's business is and the more specific the service requirements for his systems are, the higher his tendency will be to carry out O&M with own resources. For example, in car manufacturing and metallurgy, outsourcing of O&M is rather seldom. In less technical businesses, like logistics, it is quite frequent. Typically, most large airports have outsourced the O&M for their technical systems to external suppliers.

Even if some customers may consider it a non-core activity, O&M is still mission-critical for their business success. For example, if the baggage handling system of an airport is down over a longer period of time, the entire airport operation is affected. Flights are delayed, and passengers will not receive their bags at their destination. Depending on external suppliers for highly critical technical areas is always regarded by the customers as a high operational risk and a strong reason for fearing outsourcing. Thus, especially for the O&M of new systems, the first sales effort must concentrate on taking away this fear. If the customer already has an own service organization, this fear will be often nurtured by his own service people. This is for instance the case if exiting systems are already serviced by own people and the customer plans to buy an additional one. The own service employees will always regard external suppliers as potential competitors putting their jobs in jeopardy. They will try to influence the decision, obviously in their favor, whether the service for a new system should be outsourced or rendered in-house. Most times, in-house service people tend to ignore the fact that new systems are usually technically significantly more advanced than their old one and that the new service requirements may exceed their current capabilities. Talking to the customer's service people about outsourcing is the wrong address. Either the supplier finds ways to influence such a decision at the top level of the customer's organization, or he will fail. Therefore, the suppliers' top managers must take an active role in the acquisition phase of such projects. Leaving this sales effort to sales people only would be insufficient.

Before deciding to outsource the O&M for their core systems, customers require an assurance from the top management of the service company. For large contracts they want to hear that their project will be on the supplier CEO's agenda and that he or she will be ready to personally step in if a serious problem arises. Suppliers who are capable of smartly bringing their CEO in position at the right time will be more successful.

Personalizing the sales effort is a good tactic. Additionally to knowing the supplier's CEO, COO, or Head of Service, it is very important that customers can also give a face to the new project service organization. This can be accomplished by introducing the future O&M manager and maybe one or two other key people, such as the maintenance engineer or IT expert, and by actively engaging them in the sales process. It is always a proof of a supplier's solidity and reliability if he can present the future key players already in an early stage of business acquisition. Naturally, these individuals would have to demonstrate strong subject matter expertise backed up by a successful professional track record. It usually makes a strong impression on customers if the future O&M manager personally presents and sustains his service concept during negotiations. Setting up a strong virtual or fix mobilization team consisting of service managers and technical experts dedicated at supporting all important contract negotiations and project mobilizations can be very helpful in this regard.

Once the customers feel that they can trust the service provider, technical and economic factors come into focus.

For mature integrated service suppliers, sustaining the technical and organizational concept of their service offer by also addressing the specific operational requirements of the new systems should be something quite straight forward.

Dealing with the economic challenges is far more difficult. Many customers are of the opinion of already having granted their suppliers a favor by awarding them the system installation. Thus, they will often ask in return for a give-away in the area of service. This sometimes puts integrated service suppliers under great pressure. Offering customers a compromise in the area of service, like by making price reductions or by taking over additional works, as a compensation for problems incurred during system installation is a bad but still common business policy. Service managers should not accept such foul trade-ins.

If such things happen regularly, it proves that the supplier considers service only a second priority. Service managers should escalate this matter to the top level of the company and ask for clarification.

Even though system suppliers are in an advantageous position for also receiving the post-installation service and external competition plays a minor role, the price pressure on service is still high. Most customers assess a service offer on the basis of their own cost estimation. Often, they are asking for offers containing a detailed layout of the future service organization with indication of headcounts and qualifications. On this basis, they try to determine the service costs as if rendered with own people and will use this estimation to benchmark the supplier's offer against an in-house solution. A common mistake most customers make in this regard is to look at the direct personnel costs only, without considering the costs for personnel recruitment, mobilization, training, fluctuation, and administration. Labor rates for people executing commodity works requiring a lower level of qualification are very transparent. Therefore, commodity work packages should be clearly and transparently reflected in the supplier's offer cost-breakdown and should be moderately priced. High-tech packages are harder to benchmark and usually allow higher markups.

Unfortunately (for both parties), the leading role on the customers' side during negotiations is usually taken by the procurement departments, at least in the initial negotiation phases. Their main (an often only) mission is to negotiate the lowest possible price. Therefore, they will try to keep the focus of negotiations on costs. Maximizing the value for money is not their first priority, also because most procurement people do not really have the required subject matter expertise for assessing the value of service. The customers' operations people (the ones who eventually will have to cope with bad service quality) usually play a pale role and have no big influence in these meetings. If the suppliers let negotiations go down that road, they will be forced in a battle they cannot win. In fact, many times the suppliers do not succeed in directing the discussions towards the value of their services and are forced into the role of continuously having to justify their costs. In many cases, this happens due to the lack of self-confidence of the suppliers' negotiation teams. One of the reasons for such a lack of self-confidence is that senior people from the supplier are often missing in these meetings. It is essential that in the decisive negotiation rounds a senior service representative shifts the focus on value. Such value becomes most evident by looking at the costs of lost production incurred by customers as a result of bad service. More information in this regard will be provided in the chapter *The Value of Service*. Before going into contract negotiations, service people should be perfectly prepared in this regard. Many customers, and especially their procurement departments, prefer to totally ignore this aspect. They think that performance problems can be solved by including performance targets and performance related penalties in the contract terms. This is often illusory, because in most contracts the technical terms and boundary conditions are not defined precisely enough, and, therefore, smart suppliers will usually find an escape door to avoid punishment. A good tactical move suppliers could make is by suspending negotiations when they feel like hitting a wall with the procurement departments and by asking for the participation of the customers' business managers in the meeting. The negotiation teams of integrated service suppliers should be conscious of usually being the customers' preferred choice and that by awarding the service to a third party, the latter would assume a high operational risk. This should be reason enough for the suppliers to not accept being pushed around.

The situation is more complicated when the new system and the post-installation service are negotiated together. Here, most customers are looking for the combined offer with the lowest TCO. This is sometimes causing suppliers quite some headaches because they do not always have a coherent integral tactical approach covering the system installation as well as the service. Most system suppliers are organized in two separate business units, one for new systems and one for service, with each of them having its own management and its own business targets. Therefore, the danger of going into negotiations uncoordinated is high. It is the supplier CEO's role to define the common tactic. Even though the first priority will always be to sell the new system, scarifying the service blindly to accomplish this goal is the wrong tactic and will backfire later. Accepting a calculated long-term liability in the area of service to secure the winning of a strategic project is a different story. But in such a case, this matter should be internally documented and clearly reflected in the service targets.

For systems and installations companies, a good alignment and coordination between their systems and service units is essential. It shall include the definition and continuous adaptation of the joint approach and ensure the timely flow of relevant information between the two departments. It is unacceptable that service is often involved too late in the sales process and caught by surprise. Without enough lead time and without the required information regarding the system, the local market conditions, and the customer, compiling a consistent service offer is impossible.

An important parameter in the assessment of TCO based offers is the duration of the operations phase the customers are considering for the evaluation of the offer. The longer this period, the higher the service costs will be and the more important a competitive service offer becomes. Therefore, knowing this parameter as early as possible is essential for the preparation of a smart TCO offer. Often, the binding contract term is much shorter than the duration of the operations phase the customer uses to assess the TCO value of a service offer. In such a case, suppliers should risk going into negotiations with a more courageous service approach if this is required for winning the combined order. They will have the opportunity to renegotiate unfavorable contract conditions at expiration of the first binding term. Warranty is another element integrated suppliers should smartly deal with. Warranty contingencies are an important cost factor in the system offer. If the supplier is awarded also the service, warranty works could be executed at no additional labor costs because sufficient service personnel would be on site anyway. Thus, depending on the specific tactical project approach, warranty costs could either be reduced in the system offer, or part of the warranty provisions could be used later for supporting the service.

Even though a service contract may look unattractive for the supplier in the beginning, over a longer duration it will always yield enough opportunities for profit improvement. This will be explained later in more detail in the *Operations* chapter.

A potential threat sales people should always be keeping in mind is the risk of being abused. It is often the case that customers still ask for additional offers, even though they already have made their decision with regard to which supplier they really want. This is happening quite often for brown-field service

contracts. Customers use such additional offers for benchmarking purposes aimed at putting their supplier of choice under pressure. Preparing a good service concept for a large installation requires a high level of expertise and a lot of work. Therefore, it is especially frustrating if customers let one supplier work out such a concept, just to hand it over as a requirement specification to their supplier of choice. This is, by the way, also an intrinsic risk of the new systems business. Suppliers must develop their own tactic for mitigating this risk. A thorough analysis of the project background, of the competitors, and of the customer's contract award history can be of help. If, for instance, the customer has been working with one supplier over a longer period and if this supplier has succeeded in renewing the contract a couple of times, the chances for another supplier to get his foot into the door are rather low. If the contract incumbent has rendered an acceptable job, he will always have a competitive edge over the other bidders. He may have established good connections inside the customer's organization, and even relationships at personal level are often existing. A common reason why customers are re-tendering service contracts is their intention to reduce the contract price through competition. Additionally, public procurement law usually forces public customers to re-tender their service contracts regularly. A chance for a new supplier may arise if the contract incumbent has failed in developing his contract over the years by introducing new technologies and work practices or has omitted to share productivity gains with his customer.
All these parameters have to be carefully evaluated before investing into preparing an offer for a large service contract. The early engagement of the supplier's top management usually increases the commitment on the side of the customers and reduces the risk of being abused.

A sometimes still observed and extremely bad habit of some suppliers is to provide poorly prepared offers at extremely low prices just with the intention of spoiling the contract price of the winning competitor. Service managers should be smart enough to understand that such foul practices are also destroying their own market.

Suppliers should always start negotiations with the intention of building a true partnership with their customers and should do their utmost to maintain this approach over the entire duration of the contract. They should offer genuine value and expect a fair treatment in return. Those customers who do not honor such an approach will usually not be able to find a good service partner and will pay a high price in long-term.

Benjamin Franklin's quote "The bitterness of poor quality remains long after the sweetness of low price is forgotten" is still valid—today maybe even more than in his days. Systems are becoming increasingly more complex, and the consequences of poor quality are more severe. It is quite surprising to still see a certain blindness on the side of customers with regard to recognizing the immense value of good service for their business combined with the refusal of accepting that such service has its price. As a passionate tennis player, such acting reminds me of somebody who has spent a lot of money for a new tennis racket, just to spoil his or her game by playing with worn-out balls on a badly prepared court.

Competition

For integrated service suppliers, the customers' own in-house service organizations are the strongest competitor. With each new system, customers must make a strategic decision whether to outsource the service or to rather render it with own resources. If customers follow an outsourcing strategy, the integrated service supplier will always be their first choice. Awarding the service to somebody else, a generic service provider or another system supplier, entails high operational risks and is quite unusual. Even in the unlikely case that the service contract for a new system is subject to open tender, only just a few generic service providers and probably no other integrated service supplier will participate. This is especially the case for large and complex new systems. For all other suppliers, the risk stemming from proprietary systems and components as well as from technical complexity is too high. For reducing this risk, they would need support contracts from the original suppliers, which (naturally) would be hard to receive for a low price.

For encouraging competition, customers may divide their requests for proposal into commodity packages, such as mechanical and electrical, and high-tech or proprietary ones, like controls and IT. Even though genuinely preferring to have one supplier for all packages, customers are often opening competition for generic jobs mainly to discourage the original suppliers from abusing their dominant position. Such a strategy possibly attracts other players, some of them venturing themselves into competition on a 'What do we have to lose?' approach by offering their services at extremely low prices. Commodity packages are usually in the focus of generic service providers.

Sometimes, it may also happen that other integrated suppliers are bidding for generic packages. In this case, it is important to find out what their intention behind this unusual move could be. Do they have a strategic interest, or do they just want to spoil the price? Rather than panicking, the integrated service supplier must maintain his composure and pursue his tactic. It would be a great mistake to act offended or to not accept the customer's attempt of encouraging competition. Customers would only take this as a proof for having done the right thing. The supplier should signal the customer that he is taking competition serious but also that he is still convinced of being able to make the best-value-for-money offer.

Integrated suppliers still have a couple of aces up their sleeves. Knowing that there is no practical alternative to being awarded the high-tech package, they must offer this package on a stand-alone basis by considering the commodity packages only as an optional add-on. This means including the complete overhead costs, such as for management, administration, and infra-structure, into the calculation of the proprietary part and making a rock-bottom offer for the commodity one. Generic packages are easily comparable; therefore, they should be priced moderately and kept rather transparent. Because all other competitors would have to include all administration costs into their (commodity part) offer, the integrated supplier should be capable of offering an attractive price also for this package. By nature, high-tech services are less transparent, and the service effort required by complex and proprietary components is harder for the customer to assess. Maintaining a certain contingency in the high-tech package price which can be offered as a discount to the customer for awarding all works to one supplier is often a good tactic.

Customers should know that by engaging different service providers, they burden themselves with a significant additional coordination effort. For executing repair works on certain parts of the system, one supplier may need the support of another for shutting it off. If the system fails and the cause is not clear, none of the suppliers will take the initiative to solve the problem. In all these cases, the customer would have to coordinate his different suppliers. Such coordination is highly tedious and often results in all parties cross-blaming each other. Interfaces between different service packages can be rather complex, and in many situations when things go wrong, clear accountability is hard to assign.

In conclusion, as long as the customers do not get the impression that integrated service suppliers are abusing their position, they will prefer to receive all services from one hand. There are many good examples of integrated service suppliers having successfully retained their initial contracts for more than 15 years, thus becoming genuine life-cycle partners of their customers.

After the first years of operation, the criticality and relevance of proprietary components decreases. For example, if IT has been working free of trouble for a couple of years, it can be expected that it will not cause many problems in the future. This could possibly lower the entry barriers for new service providers and put the incumbent in front of new challenges. Customers who are aware that their system will sooner or later require rejuvenation works to maintain its performance are more inclined to keep the original system supplier in the loop. Therefore, integrated service suppliers should offer additional value by proposing upgrading and modernization solutions targeted at protecting their customers' investment and also at reducing the operational risk exposure related to the obsolescence of aging components.

Competition for brown-field systems service is far more intense. Apart from a couple of larger suppliers also acting internationally and capable of servicing larger and more complex systems, this market is generally dominated by smaller local companies. In their core focus are small to medium systems of rather low complexity. Their competitive advantage are low prices which they can offer by using people with rather moderate qualifications and by not always strictly adhering to labor regulations. The participation of integrated suppliers in such competition only makes sense on a selective basis, for instance if a customer's installation has strategic relevance. Such relevance could be given by pending modernization projects or by new installations the customer may be planning.

Contracts

In comparison with contracts for new systems, which are usually very precise and well elaborated, the quality of service contracts is often low. The problem starts already with the requests for proposal (RFP) issued by the customers. These RFPs are often drafted by people from the new systems faculty who do not always have extensive experience in the area of service. Often, such drafts are reused and adapted from other projects and customers, becoming increasingly unclear and sometimes containing ambiguous and even contradicting clauses.
A weak service contract may present the advantage for the supplier for interpreting it in his favor, but it will undoubtedly lead to later disputes between the two parties and thus cannot provide the basis for a good cooperation.

Contract Forms

Generally, there are three major types of contracts suited for the service business for large installations:

- Lump-sum (or fix price) contracts
- Performance based contracts
- Cost-plus contracts

In **lump-sum contracts**, the services are executed at a fix price which includes the supplier's direct costs, his administration costs, as well as his profit. Depending on the contract terms, the price may vary along the years with inflation. Because they are easier to handle, most customers prefer this type of contracts. Most procurement departments of customers are reluctant to accept other types of contracts in the tender

process. An important prerequisite for a successful lump-sum service contract is that the scope of services is clear and that an efficient mechanism for dealing with variations is established in the contract terms.
In a new partnership between customers and suppliers, lump-sum contracts are a good starting point. Both parties know exactly what they can expect from each other and there is little room for surprises. For the suppliers, this kind of contracts is advantageous because all performance improvements and cost reductions they potentially could achieve during contract execution represent additional profit. There are a couple of typical weaknesses of lump-sum contracts which need to be addressed: (1) For the customers they are totally untransparent. As a result, customers usually suspect their suppliers of earning too much profit. Such suspicion goes against a trustful customer–supplier partnership. (2) With no real motivation for enhancing the level of their services beyond what is contractually agreed and no incentive for offering customers additional value, suppliers are usually doing just as much as required to avoid penalties.

If the partnership continues over a longer period of time and is ruled by mutual trust, transforming a lump-sum contract into a performance based one could benefit both parties.

In **performance-based contracts**, the supplier's payment is linked to the fulfillment of certain performance indicators. The supplier receives the base (or reference) payment if the performance indicators defined in the performance scheme are fulfilled. For each indicator, the performance scheme defines a base (or reference) value, a maximum, and a minimum performance value. Additionally, the performance scheme also specifies the weighting of the individual performance indicators in percent (so that they sum up to 100%) and defines a mechanism for conveying the degree of fulfillment of each indicator into a monetary value. If the supplier exceeds the base value of a performance indicator, he receives a bonus over his base payment. If he fails in achieving this value, his base payment is reduced accordingly. The maximum performance values are intended for preventing that the contractors increase their performance beyond the level of economic relevance for the customer's business and also for setting an upper limit for the payment of bonuses. For example, if the customer cannot make economic use of any additional fraction of percent of system availability beyond a certain value, this value should represent the maximum performance value for availability. If the supplier performs below the base value and above the minimum performance value, his payment is reduced accordingly, but without triggering any potential additional damage claims. If his performance drops under the minimum performance value, the supplier has a serious performance issue, especially if this happens more often. In such a case, he would not only lose his complete incentive related to that particular performance indicator but would possibly also incur liquidated damages claims.

Performance based contracts generally stimulate the suppliers to continuously enhance the level of their performance. For example, a supplier would invest into a new condition monitoring (CM) system if the extra payment he receives over the remaining contract duration for improving the system re-liability exceeds his investment into the new CM system. A real win-win situation would be established if the value of extra production for the customer resulting from the higher system reliability exceeds the additional incentive-related payments to his supplier.

Most mature customer–supplier relationships are founded on performance-based contracts. There are a couple of typical success factors which, if embraced by both parties, can lead to a successful win-win situation. Performance based contracts need time to develop. Therefore, the duration of such contracts must be rather long, at least five years or more. Frequently changing the suppliers makes it impossible to implement such contracts. The parties need to agree upon a meaningful performance scheme. It should include only performance indicators of genuine economic value for the customer's business. The performance thresholds must be challenging and fair. Ideally, the performance scheme is jointly developed by both parties during live system operation. Therefore, agreeing on a 'wear-in' period, as it will be explained later in this chapter, can be very helpful. The performance indicators must reflect the real operational requirements of the customer's business. As these requirements may change in time, the performance scheme should be adapted regularly, usually on an annual basis.

A methodology for introducing an incentive scheme into a performance based contract is presented in the *Appendix*.

In **cost-plus contracts**, the suppliers are reimbursed for all their costs (direct and administration) and receive an agreed level of profit on top. Such contracts require an open-book policy in which the suppliers provide a complete and transparent overview of all their costs. At first sight, such contracts seem attractive for the suppliers, because the cost risk is zero. The downside is that in these contracts the profits are usually low because customers only accept very moderate mark-ups on top of the costs. For the customers, the downside of cost-plus contracts is that these contracts do not provide any incentive for the suppliers for trying to reduce costs. It can be often observed

that the volume of such contracts continuously grows over the years. This type of contract is only suitable for projects where the scope of works cannot be clearly defined.
Cost-based (open book) contracts in combination with a performance incentive scheme can be an interesting alternative though. This is the only form of contracts that allows the sharing of cost improvement benefits between suppliers and customers. In lump-sum contracts, only the supplier benefits from such improvements. In pure cost-plus contracts, the supplier has no interest to reduce costs. Defining project costs as one of the performance indicators in the incentive scheme of such a cost-based performance-oriented contract solves this dilemma. The target costs are mutually agreed on a yearly basis and represent the reference value for the cost indicator. Staying below this target means that the supplier receives part of these savings as an incentive. Conversely, if the costs target is exceeded, this would imply a reduction of his base profit.

Performance Indicators

In the systems and installations business, performance indicators generally describe certain levels of performance a system is expected to achieve during operation. Performance indicators fall into the following two main categories: operational and technical.

Operational indicators describe the process related system capabilities, such as throughput, production capacity, or energy consumption. They are mainly system-intrinsic and fall primarily into the responsibility of the system manufacturer.

Technical indicators are more related to the boundary conditions under which the end-users can expect their systems to operate.

Common examples for technical indicators are the **system availability** and the **system reliability**.

The *system availability* is defined as the percentage of time a system is able to perform during a specific reference time period. For example, the reference period for the daily availability could be 24 hours, or it could also be defined as just the 16 hours of peak operation time. In the latter case, a system stop of 30 minutes would mean a loss of availability of approximately 3%, while in the former case the loss would be only 2%. Obviously, the shorter the reference period for availability is selected, the harder it is to compensate failures during this period. A longer downtime may not affect the monthly performance but it will probably jeopardize the daily availability target. Therefore, it is very important to precisely specify this reference period and also to define whether the unavailability of a system or component in periods when these items are not required to operate is considered relevant for the system availability calculation.
The *system reliability* defines the ability of a system to work free of trouble over a specific period of operation. It can be measured by the *Mean Time Between Failures* (MTBF) or by the number of system failures in a specific period of time. Obviously, the higher the MTBF or the lower the number of failures is, the more reliably the system functions. The technical performance of a system, as measured by its availability or reliability, is influenced by several factors. It is not only determined by the intrinsic capabilities of the system but is also largely depending on the quality of service and on the way the customer operates it.

Additionally, to the above-mentioned operational and technical indicators, there are also indicators primarily intended for measuring the performance of service providers as well as the quality of their services. The most common such indicator is the *response time* to service calls. It defines the period between the time a problem was reported and the time the service provider starts working on it. In a service contract this indicator could be defined as follows: 'The supplier is expected to attend minimum 90% of the service calls in less than 30 minutes.' Another such indicator is the *restoration time* in which the supplier is expected to restore the system operation after a failure. These indicators are primarily used in support contracts and are less relevant in O&M contracts with on-site presence of the service provider.

In the technical sections, most service contracts focus too much on system availability. Unless very precisely described, this parameter is often meaningless. For example, a monthly system availability of 99% offers little customer value if the system goes down twice for 2 hours during peak operation time. Even though such failure would really hurt the customer's business, by assuming a 7 days per week operation and a daily operation window of 15 hours, the system would still have solidly performed above contractual requirements. On the other hand, if a component is not needed at a specific time or if a redundant one could be used instead, its unavailability does not have any operational relevance. For large systems with many components, the availability is difficult to define and calculate. It can be easily assessed at component level but is very hard to meaningfully determine at system level.

For customers, the system reliability and operational performance during peak operation periods are more important. Using the airport example again, the percentage of bags arriving in due time at their destination inside the baggage system would be a very useful performance indicator. Similarly, the reliable operation of this system during the morning and evening peaks, when most flights leave and arrive, would also be of great relevance.

As mentioned before, the operational performance does not depend on the service quality only. This is something service providers must always keep in mind. They can work on the quality of their service, but they cannot influence the intrinsic capabilities of systems or the way customers operate them. Therefore, operational indicators are quite difficult to handle in practice. A bag at the airport may be late because the baggage process is stopped due to a system failure, but it could also be late because it was introduced too late into the system by check-in or because it was out of gauge and got stuck somewhere in the system. Excellent service cannot compensate the fact that a system may not be capable of achieving certain performance levels or may frequently fail because it was badly designed. Defining clear boundary conditions under which service can ensure the required performance levels is of major importance. If the system does not possess the intrinsic capability of yielding a certain technical or operational performance, there is nothing service can do. If the system as well as the pertaining service were procured from the same supplier, this should obviously not be the customer's concern; the supplier must solve the problem, regardless of its cause. Installations companies should define a clear internal segregation of responsibility in this regard. If the system has deficiencies, these problems must be corrected by the systems units and should not be transferred to service.

Most customers link service quality to the fulfillment of contractual performance indicators such as availability and system throughput. This approach is incomplete though. One aspect customers usually do not have on their radar screen is the preservation of the good **technical condition of their systems**, thus the long-term protection of their investment. Practice shows that for a while a system may still be capable of yielding the required performance even though important maintenance works are not executed properly and the system condition is continuously degrading. Many weak service providers are speculating on this fact and offer low quality services at very low prices. This happens especially in the case of brown-field services contracts which are frequently re-tendered and have a short contract duration (one to three years) and where participation is open also to suppliers with unproven capabilities. Many customer procurement departments are falling into this trap. Even though it may require some extra costs, the regular assessment of the technical system condition should be part of any consistent service contract. All good maintenance practitioners with experience in the respective industry should be able to complete such an assessment with manageable effort. Quality service suppliers should have developed standardized procedures for conducting such an assessment and for making the system condition measurable and quantifiable. Alternatively, it could be contractually agreed that a third-party expert is contracted for conducting such a system condition assessment on a regular base. Customers should actively ask the suppliers during negotiations about their policy with regard to preserving the good technical condition of the systems they service.

Unfortunately, too much time is spent in negotiations on meaningless and minor details like decimal percent fractions of system availability. A proven method for terminating such useless discussions would be to ask the customers about the real monetary value for their business resulting from a system availability increase of 0.x%. In most cases, this question would be as difficult for most customers to answer as it would be for the suppliers to assess the additional effort required for providing the same amount of extra system availability.

Actually, asking exactly this question during the renegotiation of a major service contract helped me in terminating some tedious endless discussions regarding the system availability. Our customer (an airport operator) was adamantly requiring an overall system availability of 99%. Knowing that for the past term the contractually agreed target for this KPI was 98.5% and reaching this level was already quite challenging, occasionally even triggering minor liquidated damages, I continued insisting on the 98.5%. As at that time only the purchasing department of the customer was present in the negotiations and the discussions got stuck at this point, I asked for speaking to the customer's COO before continuing. After explaining the situation, I asked him directly what these additional 0.5% monetarily meant for his business and indicated that this would substantially increase our service fee. As expected, he could not provide a concrete answer to this question. After asking again why they then kept insisting on the 99%, he eventually told me that it was his intention of conveying this value to *his* customer (an airline) as a proof of his striving for continuous improvement and operational excellence. I told him that our service organization would of course support him in this regard, but agreeing with the 99% would expose us to potential damage claims beyond the level I was prepared to accept. Eventually, he proposed that if I accepted the 99% availability target, he would be prepared to significantly reduce the levels of liquidated damages. Since this solution would not have increased our risk exposure, and because I also was confident that our service technicians would do their best in this regard, I agreed. Thus, by understanding each other's goals, we were able to achieve an agreement which set the foundation for a continued good collaboration and for another successful contract term.

In conclusion, for complex systems, technical and operational performance parameters are not easy to define. Ideally, customers and suppliers should cooperate in selecting the right indicators and in developing a meaningful performance scheme oriented toward customer value and service quality.

Supplier's Liability

The liability of suppliers is another usually strongly disputed subject during contract negotiations. There are several contractual instruments which the customers can employ to stimulate the suppliers for rendering a good job and to 'punish' them for bad performance. Such legal terms generally fall into the categories of liquidated damages, penalties, incidental, direct and consequential damages, and their practical application varies across the different country laws, local business cultures, and customer preferences.

Liquidated Damages and ***Penalties*** are instruments intended as a blanket compensation of customers for losses incurred by them as a result of a supplier's failure to fulfill certain contract terms. As the customers do not have to prove such losses, the process is much simplified. In the service business for large installations, liquidated damages or penalties are most often the consequence of not fulfilling certain technical or operational parameters, like system availability and system throughput. For example, the contract could stipulate that the contractor loses

1% of his monthly payment for each 0,1% below the required monthly system availability of 98%. Additionally, regarding performance levels, the contract may also define conditions for which the service supplier is considered to be in default, such as falling under a minimum threshold of system availability (for example 95%) or falling repetitively under a certain availability value in a specific period of time. This means that the customer may terminate the contract for missed performance. Liquidated damages should roughly reflect the real losses incurred by the customer and are not intended for being abused to artificially reduce a supplier's payment. Should this kind of compensation significantly exceed the real losses, it would have to be considered a penalty. In many county laws, penalties are not allowed; therefore, they cannot be applied.

Quality suppliers should not worry too much about liquidated damages. They usually have a good understanding of the potential magnitude of such damages and also generally can control their risk exposure in this regard, as it will be explained later. Most customers will not abuse these instruments and are rather reluctant to employ punitive measures against their suppliers if they are generally satisfied with the service quality. Mature suppliers should be able to establish a good level of cooperation with the customers' operations people and solve disputes in a constructive manner, thus making punishment obsolete. Suppliers should openly ask during negotiations how the customers have determined performance criteria and damage levels. The answers could indicate where the customers are setting their priorities and give the suppliers valuable hints on how to structure their services. It is also recommended to evaluate the level of potential liquidated damages on the basis of the expected contract profit. Accepting a 2% of potential liquidated damages in a 9% profit contract seems reasonable.

Incurring liquidated damages claims every now and then usually does not represent a serious problem for the supplier. If this occurs regularly, it is either a sign that the supplier is having serious performance issues which he must correct or is an indication that the contract terms are not achievable. Generally interested in maintaining a good working relationship with their suppliers, most customers will agree to renegotiate such inappropriate terms.

Liquidated damages are usually defined as in between 5% and 20% of the monthly payment, and for suppliers it is strongly recommended to have them capped in aggregate for the entire contract duration, for instance at 10% of the total contract value. It is quite surprising that many customers and suppliers discuss extensively about these values without having a clear understanding what they mean for their business. Performance criteria, performance thresholds and damage levels are often set arbitrarily and do not reflect the real operational requirements of the customer's business. Such values are often taken over from other contracts and may be completely unsuitable in the new context. In most contracts, precise performance measurement procedures, the related data sources, and other boundary conditions are not properly defined.

Because precise procedures regarding the measurement of performance as well as the handling of penalties usually are not available at the end of negotiations or at the beginning of a contract, it is recommended that both parties agree on a 'wear-in' period of 3 to 6 months before these mechanisms become contractually relevant. During this trial period, the performance measurement can be fine-tuned and performance indicators can be checked for appropriateness and adapted accordingly if they prove unrealistic, unfair, or not target-oriented. Generally, performance targets should be defined to stimulate the suppliers for achieving and possibly exceeding them and not to be perceived as a permanent menace. An important aspect, especially relevant for brown-field services, is whether or not the system has the intrinsic capabilities for performing according to the contractually stipulated levels (provided that service is executed correctly). An unstable IT will always generate problems no matter how much attention the service supplier is paying to it. Some systems are in bad technical condition, and this cannot always be detected during just a short site visit as usually enabled by customers during offer preparation. Therefore, when the service contract starts, many parameters may still be unclear. A trial period would open ways for addressing such deficiencies and for establishing a common and well-accepted understanding regarding performance and the handling of penalties. Additionally, suppliers should insist on introducing a clause stipulating that contractual damages become relevant only under the premises that the system is really capable of operating at the required performance levels. Such a clause is especially important in brown-field contracts for third-party systems. In green-field service projects for own systems such clause would not be appropriate and, understandably, would irritate the customers.

Incidental, direct and consequential damages are a greater concern for suppliers because the related risk exposure is more difficult to assess. The potential damage a customer may argue to have incurred could be completely disproportionate to the value of a service contract. For not exposing themselves to incalculable risks, it is very important that customers and suppliers understand the exact meaning as well as the differences between these three kinds of damages. To be liable for such damages, a party has to be in default. This is an essential difference from liquidated damages.

Incidental damages are all the costs incurred by the non-breaching party in the attempt to avoid further damages, such as direct or consequential ones, resulting from a contract breach of the other party. Undertaking the possible to mitigate the consequences of a failure of one party is a mandatory pre-requisite for the other party to be able to claim compensation for further damages.

Direct (general) damages are damages which can be considered the natural and necessary result of a contract breach and are likely to occur in any similar contract.

"*Direct damages* means those damages which naturally and necessarily flow from a wrongful act, are so usual an accompaniment of the kind breach alleged that the mere allegation of the breach gives sufficient notice, and are conclusively presumed to have been foreseen or contemplated by the party as a consequence of his breach."[1]

Consequential (special) damages are damages beyond the two above-mentioned categories. As such, they are not the usual result of a contract breach but are instead attributable to certain special circumstances of the non-breaching party.

"The distinction between general [or direct] and special [or consequential] damages is [...] that general [or direct] damages are such as naturally and ordinarily follow the breach, whereas

---

[1] *Carlisle Corp. v. Med. City Dallas, Ltd., 196 S.W.3d 855 (Tex. App.-Dallas, 2006)*

whereas special [or consequential] damages are those that ensue, not necessarily or ordinarily, but because of special circumstances"[2]

For being eligible to receive a compensation for any incidental, direct, or consequential damages, (1) the non-breaching party must prove that the damage was actually incurred, (2) must prove that the damage resulted from a wrongful act committed by the breaching party, and (3) for both parties, these damages must be the reasonably foreseeable result of such wrong-doing.

Distinguishing between direct and consequential damages is not always straightforward, because it requires determining whether the damage was the natural result of a wrongful act or is rather attributable to special circumstances on the side of the claiming party.

The following hypothetical example from the airport industry shall provide guidance in this regard.

The peak handling capacity of the baggage handling system in a larger airport is around 30,000 to 50,000 bags per day. If the system is down for two hours during peak time, maybe 10,000 bags could be delayed, and maybe 5,000 bags would be left behind (miss the airplane). This means that many passengers would have to fly out without their bags. If this system downtime is the result of negligence, such as by a wrongful service activity, the service supplier is in default and therefore liable for all resulting damages.

---

[2] Applied Data Processing, Inc. v. Burroughs Corp., 394 F. Supp. 504, 509 (D. Conn., 1975)

For mitigating the consequences of such failure, the airport operator may decide to bring in additional baggage handlers for removing stray bags from the baggage system and thus allow that these bags can be reprocessed faster once the operation of the baggage system is restored. These costs incurred by the customer fall into the category of *incidental damages.*

Bags which have missed their flight need to be reprocessed. This means re-funneling them through the baggage system, sending them to their destination on another flight, and finally bringing them to their owner by taxi. The total costs for reprocessing such left behind bags are around 100 Euros per piece. In our example, the total costs would sum up to the significant amount of 5,000 bags x 100 Euros/bag = 500,000 Euros. As these costs are a direct and natural result of a faulty service activity causing the baggage system failure and can be expected to occur in every similar service contract, they belong into the category of *direct damages*.

The majority of these costs would usually have to be borne by the airlines. If the airport terminal is operated directly by the airline (as it is the case in many US airports), the liability of the service provider is straightforward: As long as the liability for direct damages is not excluded in the service contract, he must compensate the airline for these losses. If the BHS is operated by the airport, the situation is more complicated. As there a contract between these two parties does not exist, the airline cannot directly claim (based on contract law) for compensation by the service provider. Instead, depending on the terms of its contract with the airport, the airline could ask for compensation by the latter, for instance in the form of liquidated damages (100 Euros/left behind bag). This example introduces the additional aspect of damages incurred by third parties. If the contract between the airport and the service provider does not waive indemnification for third-party claims, the airport could pass on these damages to the latter. From the perspective of the service supplier, this claim would fall into the category of consequential damages—as explained in the next paragraph.

Any damages which are not a natural consequence of the baggage system failure, for instance could be attributed to the special circumstances resulting from the terms of the contract between the airport and the airline, fall into the category of *consequential damages*. Damages resulting from a potential loss of reputation on the side of the airport or the airline would also fall into this category.

Lost profits do not necessarily fall into the category of consequential damages. If such lost profits of one party are the natural result of the failure of the other party—like in the case of lost production (equaling to lost revenues and profits) due to a system failure caused by the service provider—these damages may be considered as direct.

Different from liquidated damages, a service supplier is liable for incidental, direct, or consequential damages only if he is in default, for example, if he is responsible for a faulty service activity or has neglected to carry out a required task.

The burden of proof in such a case lies with the customer. Often, such proof is quite difficult to provide though.

Regarding the liability for direct and consequential damages, a well-balanced contract should also consider the nature of a supplier's failure. For example, US law and German law are distinguishing between gross and simple negligence. Sending a technician to complete a critical job like an IT update for which he or she does not have the required qualifications would have to be considered a gross negligence. If a technician with the appropriate knowledge makes an error, this act would only be considered a simple negligence. While a supplier's liability for damages as a result of gross negligence or willful misconduct should be very high or even unlimited, liability for simple negligence should be capped at reasonable levels.

A false understanding regarding incidental, direct, and consequential damages can be often observed on both sides during negotiations. Many customers adamantly insist on the supplier's liability for such damages because they regard it as a general insurance against all operational losses related to their system. On the other side, suppliers are extremely afraid of such liability because they consider it a sort of general imprisonment for whatever goes wrong with the installation. Both assumptions are incorrect. For example, if a component fails even though all required maintenance tasks were executed correctly, the service supplier would not be in default. Thus, he would not be liable for any incidental, direct, or consequential damages resulting from this system failure. The trigger for such a liability is a supplier's default in conjunction with a system failure. It is not the failure itself. However, the customer may claim for liquidated damages if such the contract allows such claims.

IT is a well-suited example to illustrate this topic. In most large modern installations, IT is the most critical component. If the IT system goes down, usually the whole operation is stopped. IT failures can never be totally avoided. Software as well as most hardware components are not subject to wear and have a rather random failure pattern. Service suppliers cannot totally prevent IT failures. The only thing they can do is to diligently carry out all required inspections and preventive maintenance tasks and to implement suitable measures and procedures for mitigating the consequences of such failures. Ensuring the on-stock availability of critical spare parts, setting up efficient software backup procedures, and having support contracts at hand with the original software and hardware suppliers would be such mitigation measures. By implementing these measures (not a complete list), the service supplier would avoid being in default in the event of IT system failures. To further reduce the operational risk stemming from IT failures, customers would have to invest into fail-safe hardware and redundant systems.

Contracts usually define specific conditions in which the supplier is considered of being in default. Such conditions arise when the supplier significantly fails in fulfilling his contractual obligations. For example, the contract may specify that if the (daily) system availability drops below a certain threshold, this is considered a severe incidence, and if such an incidence occurs more than three times in one month, the supplier would be in default. In this situation, the customer would issue a Note of Default and usually (but not necessarily) grant the supplier a certain period of time ("grace period") to fix the problem. If the supplier fails in implementing an acceptable solution, the customer may claim for incurred damages, such as direct or consequential ones.
For avoiding any ambiguity regarding this sensitive topic, suppliers should insists that contract clauses defining breach or default must contain the specification: "... for causes attributable to the supplier."

Especially for complex systems that are mission-critical for the operation of their business, customers should put a lot of emphasis on choosing a service provider with appropriate qualification. On the other side, service suppliers should be aware that by using technicians with insufficient skills, by neglecting to have support contracts for proprietary components with the original suppliers, or by insufficiently stocking critical spare parts, they are in jeopardy of being in default and thus of being exposed to high risks with regard to their liability for damages. Customers need to be aware that by requiring the acceptance of high liabilities, they act against strong suppliers and in favor of weaker ones. Small limited liability companies accept unlimited liability clauses more easily because if such liabilities materialize, they could eventually close their business. There is nothing customers could do to recover their losses. This is something premium suppliers obviously cannot do. Instead, they will include higher risk contingencies or additional insurance fees in their calculations and will thus increase the price of their offers.

When customers and suppliers negotiate the terms of their contract, it is essential that both parties share the same understanding about damages, liability and risks. It can be often observed that parties spend more time arguing about terms and conditions than on discussing the technical contents of a contract. With each party trying to be 'smarter' than the other, contract terms and conditions often become unnecessarily complex and ambiguous and provide little support for efficiently solving potential disputes during operation.

In many service projects, the liability for damages can be disproportionate to the value of the contract and especially to the achievable profits. Therefore, service providers must seek to reduce their risk exposure in this regard. From a contractual perspective, the following list of measures can be used as an orientation:

- ➔ Making liquidated damages the sole remedy for damages associated with delay or performance;
- ➔ Including a waiver for direct and consequential damages or, if this is not acceptable for the customer, including a limitation for such damages in aggregate and, if possible, also per event;
- ➔ Including a waiver for damage claims of third parties;
- ➔ Agreeing on a trial period at the beginning of the contract, before damages become contractually relevant.

The more precisely the contract specifies the concrete damages for which the supplier is liable, the less it will give reason for later disputes between the two parties, which eventually need to be settled in court. The high complexity of the liability topic makes thorough legal support for the drafting of service contracts and during contract negotiations indispensable.

If customers and suppliers understand above-mentioned aspects, they can jointly agree on fair, motivating, and rewarding contract terms to the benefit of both parties.

Other Aspects

Aging components may expose service providers to substantial technical risks. Especially in long-term contracts, such components may start failing repeatedly, may require excessive repair work and even become un-maintainable, for instance if spare parts cannot be procured any longer. This risk can be mitigated by conducting a thorough technical system condition assessment before engaging into a new contract term.

Obsolescence is an aspect which often leads to disputes between customers and suppliers. Even though all regular maintenance tasks are carried out with the required care, some components may degrade to the point that they are not in a maintainable condition and cannot function reliably any longer. In this case, they need an upgrade, overhaul or modernization. A good example are IT systems (software and hardware), which need to be upgraded regularly. As it will be addressed in more detail in the chapter *The Value of Service*, the original suppliers are discontinuing the service of older systems and are requiring an upgrade to the latest software and hardware versions. Mechanical and electrical parts can also fall into this category and may require a major overhaul after a certain period of time. A further obsolescence problem may arise when certain spare parts are not available any longer and require the development of substitutes.

A good contract must precisely define which of these tasks are part of the regular service scope (and thus included in the maintenance budget) and which works need to be carried out as separate projects for which the customer must allocate an extra budget.

Large O&M contracts require a high number of service people, sometimes several hundred. Therefore, the development of personnel costs in long-term service contracts is an aspect of high relevance. Usually, customers insist that the suppliers alone bear this risk and ask for firm fix prices including inflation, sometimes for more than 10 years and spanning over several (binding) contract prolongation options. Because of the general aversion of both parties of being exposed to such uncontrollable risk, negotiations regarding this aspect are usually difficult and tedious. Customers feel uncomfortable with floating prices also because it makes budgeting more difficult. For these reasons, they adamantly insist on fix prices and disqualify deviating

offers. A good practice in this regard, even though the customer may not be asking for it, is to make the inflation related markup transparent and to present two prices, a net one and another one including inflation. Making this markup transparent usually yields the chance for openly discussing this issue during negotiations. Customers should be aware that suppliers will usually reduce the quality of their services to compensate potential financial gaps resulting from an incorrect assessment of the labor market development. Therefore, customers should know the markup used by the different suppliers and should be rather concerned with too aggressive offers in this regard. Because the development of local labor costs cannot be influenced neither by the customers nor by the suppliers, sharing this risk seems fair. An appropriate solution would be to link the personnel related portion of the contract to an index reflecting the local labor cost development. National statistics usually provide such information. Though, in dynamic markets, such statistics are not always accurate and reliable.
In a tight situation when winning a contract is at jeopardy because the parties cannot agree on inflation, suppliers should accept a calculated risk by setting inflation in their calculations 'on the edge' and by compensating potential future gaps through productivity gains. A compromise could be made by agreeing on a certain threshold for the annual inflation rate, beyond which the customer would have to absorb the additional costs.

In many cases, customers are asking for an integral offer including the system as well as the service, in which the latter is an option that can be ordered at a later time. One possible reason why customers are not ordering the service together with the system could be that they want more time to decide whether to outsource the service or to rather execute it with own people. Another reason could also be their fear of letting the supplier off the hook too early. Thus, they prefer to keep something in the back of their hands which they can use to put the suppliers under pressure, for instance by asking for concessions in the area of service as a compensation for potential inconveniences and dissatisfaction experienced during system installation. Usually, the service contract award happens very late and often does not leave enough time for a proper project mobilization. Thus, suppliers should insist on contractually fixing the latest date for the award of the service contract. For large service projects, a lead time of minimum six months should be agreed on.

A good contract should also specify the boundary conditions for performing the services and should also define how deviations are to be handled. Such conditions are, for example, the operating pattern and the system utilization. For service, it is important that enough maintenance windows are specified in the contract and that later during operation these windows are made available. The level of system utilization is also relevant. If the installation needs to perform regularly above the planned performance levels, it will be subject to higher wear and tear, thus requiring more spare parts and service hours. The contract should specify how this extra effort is remunerated. On the other hand, the installation may sometimes be not needed at its full capacity, and certain parts could even be shut off. If such a situation persists over a longer period of time, customers will usually ask for a reduction of the service price. A recent example for such an event is the Corona pandemic, which has drastically hit airports and airlines.
The better the contract addresses above-mentioned aspects, the less it will give reason for later disputes between customers and suppliers.

A comprehensive, consistent, and fair service contract is a mandatory prerequisite for a good customer–supplier relationship. Nevertheless, many service contracts do not fulfill these requirements. Instead of fostering the cooperation between customers and their suppliers and of establishing a true win-win situation, many contracts make the two parties perceive themselves rather as opponents in a battle which only one can win.

Two frequent reasons for such bad contracts are:

(1) Many requests for proposal and also contracts are drafted by people who are specialized on the installations business and are not well enough familiar with service. Such contracts are often copy-pasted from one application to the other, getting increasingly complex, inconsistent, and unclear. The unavailability of a generally accepted standard for service contracts, reflecting the specific aspects of a particular industry, is a great shortcoming in this regard.

(2) Operational people of customers are not intensively enough engaged in the development and negotiation process of service contracts. During this process, the purchasing departments of customers usually have the leading role. As a result, the contract price becomes the main (and sometimes only) argument, and therefore many of these contracts do not reflect the real operational requirements of the installations and the business needs of the customers. Typical weaknesses of such contracts are inappropriate performance indicators, unrealistic performance targets, and the lacking of a meaningful incentive scheme. On the other hand, these aspects are essential for measuring the service quality and for providing the suppliers with an incentive for improving their contribution to their

customers' business. As a result, many service contracts have a difficult start.

For ensuring the success of both parties, customers and suppliers must cooperate with the aim of establishing a win-win situation. A fair and consistent contract is indispensable in this regard.

Customer Relationship

A good customer relationship based on mutual trust is important in any business. In service, it is mission-critical. Service contracts have a long duration, and a bad relationship between customers and suppliers can induce a lot of friction, wasting efforts on both sides. As stated earlier, it is essential for service suppliers to maintain their business base by renewing their running contracts. A good customer relationship significantly increases the chances and at the same time reduces the effort required for a contract renewal. For comprehensive service contracts such as the O&M for large systems, a good customer relationship should be established at the following three levels: operational, site, and business level.

At operational level, the supplier's technicians need to establish a good cooperation with the customer's operational people—the ones who run the system. The employees of the supplier have to always be respectful and offer their support whenever possible. A 'not my job' attitude must be avoided by all means. To the contrary, especially if it does not cause any additional costs, support shall be proactively offered and the service project manager informed accordingly. It is the job of the project manager and his or her team leaders to make sure that such support is directed towards building a good relationship at operational level and that it is not abused by the customer. For the suppliers, such a good relationship at shop floor can be very advantageous. Technical failures can always occur. In this case, the customer's operational people can help to mitigate the failure consequences and possibly to avoid penalties. Making the system available for maintenance activities is a common challenge in most large service contracts. Such maintenance windows are usually limited by the operational requirements of the system. In a good contract, they are clearly defined. But often, they are too short. Sometimes, it is still possible to extend these windows by smartly adapting the production process, for example by rerouting the process flow, for making parts of the system available for maintenance. The customer's operational people will go this extra mile if their relationship with the supplier is good. In successful contracts, people on both sides perceive themselves as one team pursuing the common goal of ensuring the customer's business success. Such an ideal situation is the result of a dedicated and sustained effort on both sides.

The relationship at site level between the supplier's project/contract manager and his or her peer on the side of the customer, usually the manager responsible for the operation of the system, is the most important. If this relationship is ruled by mutual trust and respect, this spirit will also spread across both organizations, setting the foundation for a good global cooperation. Many service projects have a difficult start because suppliers and customers see themselves as opponents. Some customers feel that for the money they pay, they must squeeze out as much effort as possible from the suppliers. On the other side, many suppliers are determined to do as little as possible in order to save costs and just as much as sufficient to avoid punishment. This bad spirit usually emerges already during contract negotiations if the parties cannot agree on a fair contract. It is essential that at the beginning of a service contract, the project manager of the supplier makes the first step toward the customer for discussing the principles of the future cooperation. Taking the initiative is especially important if the contract starts under bad conditions, for instance as a result of a poor job rendered by the supplier during installation.

Sometimes, the project managers may initially run against locked doors. In this case, they must ask their superior, usually the head of the supplier's service department, for support.

An important project management task is to assess the customer satisfaction on a regular basis. This should start already during the weekly operational meetings. Project managers should explicitly ask their customers how they rate the service quality and where things possibly need to be improved. Additionally, a formalized Customer Satisfaction Review shall be conducted on a yearly basis. Such a review is carried out as a guided interview following a standardized procedure between the project manager and the customer's representative who is responsible for the system, for example the site manager. It should address various aspects including service quality, cooperation, responsiveness, pro-activity, and degree of identification with the customer's business. Each aspect must be rated on a fix scale (from innocence to excellence), thus allowing to compare results from one year to the other. For large service contracts, this is the only method of proven value. Ascertaining the customer satisfaction at generic level, such as through mailings or interviews conducted by external consultants, is completely unsuitable for this kind of business.

A good relationship at business level between the supplier's head of service and the customer's head of operations (COO) is also very important, especially when problems arise. This is, for instance, often the case if good cooperation at project level cannot be established and problems are unnecessarily escalated to the next level. The two business managers need to share the common understanding that, with regard to their own success, they depend on each other and that they have to join efforts to overcome problems. In this regard, it is essential that both

managers guide their subordinates at site level towards a trustful cooperation.
Service business managers often neglect to build a trustful relationship with their peers on the customers' side. They do not recognize the importance of a strong personal bonding with the customer at their level and usually leave this task to the project managers. As a result, the latter are often left alone. Sometimes, their manages even turn against them just to avoid a confrontation with the customers. Such an attitude maneuvers suppliers into a defensive role and weakens their position.
Good service managers show in front of their customers that they trust and stand behind their project managers and their people, but at the same time expect them to always give their best possible effort for ensuring the business success of their customers. For larger contracts, service managers should visit project sites at least on a yearly basis. This way, they demonstrate their interest for the customer's business and also for their own people. During this visit, they should also briefly discuss the results of the latest annual Customer Satisfaction Review with the customer's site manager. This feedback at site level will be very useful for the discussions that should follow with the customer's operations and business managers. By showing that they are familiar with the operational aspects of the project, service managers can build trust and empathy with their peers on the customer side.

Operations

A successful and sustainable service business must fulfill the following two conditions: It must produce genuine customer value, and it must generate profits. Good contracts in which technical and commercial aspects are properly reflected are an essential prerequisite. Other than that, the success is determined at operational level.

Contract Management

Service contracts are valuable business assets and need to be managed accordingly. Generally, contract management has three objectives: (1) improving the contract profitability, (2) retaining and renewing contracts, and (3) developing contracts. For reaching these objectives, the project/contract managers have a decisive role. Many aspects of contact management like business protection, sales, and customer relationship management have already been covered in the previous chapters.

Improving the contract profitability means constantly working at the *organizational efficiency* and the *operational effectiveness* of a service project. These two elements are the foundation of operational excellence and are closely linked to *continuous improvement*. Operational excellence is not a static condition. It is a permanently moving target. In a first step, operational excellence must be implemented by design when the project is mobilized. During operation, continuous improvement is the appropriate instrument for taking operational excellence to superior levels.

Organizational Efficiency

In essence, organizational efficiency means completing the required set of tasks with the leanest possible personnel set-up. In service, this translates in most cases to also completing the job at lowest possible costs. In large resident service contacts, the total costs are mainly (usually between 70% and 90%)[1] personnel related. 'Saving' one service technician out of twenty can already significantly improve the contract profit. Personnel redundancies shall be generally avoided. They should be only accepted as a means for increasing the organizational robustness if this is required. Making technicians fit for executing a broader spectrum of activities though cross-trade training is a proven method for increasing the organizational efficiency. Another important aspect in this regard is the balance between skills level and labor rates. People with lower skills are cheaper but usually less efficient. In large resident service contracts, most shop-floor activities are of lower technical complexity for which committed and motivated persons even with a lower level of initial professional education can acquire the required set of skills. Therefore, a good approach is to hire people with lower skills and to train them on the job. This also has the advantage that people can grow inside the organization and will thus develop a stronger identification with the project. Defining clear job roles and responsibilities and providing opportunities for professional development are further important requirements of organizational efficiency.

---

[1] depending on the local labor cost rates, the share of spare parts, mobilization costs, rents, etc.

Operational Effectiveness

Operational effectiveness means doing the right things and doing things right.

Doing the right things means executing only service activities with a proven added value for the system. This starts with properly defining the maintenance strategy and precisely describing the individual maintenance tasks regarding technical content, frequency, and required skills. Service strategies should be defined on the basis of a clear cost–benefit evaluation. Currently, a big hype is made about predictive strategies. Even though such strategies are not suitable for all types of systems, everybody seems to consider applying them as a matter of professional competence. On the other hand, run-to-failure strategies are often regarded as old-fashioned and outdated even though they can be very cost-efficient and perfectly suitable for many systems. An example for maintenance activities of little value are inspections of components with random failure pattern. Even though most inspections are concluded with no findings, the component still could fail without a warning. Following a wrong maintenance strategy results in wasted effort, unnecessary costs, and poor technical results. More details on this topic will be provided in the *Technology and Innovation* chapter.

Maintenance tasks have to be properly managed. They have to be executed as scheduled, and their results need to be documented and analyzed. In this regard, Computerized Maintenance Management Systems (CMMS) are the perfect tool. Additionally to ensuring the consistent execution of maintenance activities, the CMMS also provides valuable decision support information, such as activity reports, failure patterns, and statistical data. Defining the appropriate maintenance strategy and tasks, analyzing failure root causes, and continuously developing and improving maintenance plans is mission-critical. These tasks fall into the responsibility of the Maintenance Engineer. Therefore, he or she can be considered the brain of a service project. Many project managers fail in understanding the importance of this role and are often staffing this important position with mediocre people.

Other important elements of operational effectiveness are clear Escalation Procedures and Standard Operating Procedures (SOP). These procedures are especially relevant in emergency situations. For example, if a system goes down because of the failure of a critical component like IT, escalation procedures need to precisely describe who and in which sequence is to be informed or brought on site. It is especially important that customers are informed in due time. Escalation procedures also regulate the external support form specialists located in the central service departments or from the original equipment suppliers. Complex tasks, like the back-up or the restoration of an IT system, shall be performed according to standardized procedures. For predefined operational situations, these standard operating procedures must clearly describe the specific working steps and the sequence in which they have to be executed. They should be previously tested for completeness and effectiveness. Good escalation and standard operating procedures are essential prerequisites for mitigating the consequences of failures. Regular drills will make sure that everything functions well when required.

Doing things right means executing the service activities with all due professional care. It also means doing them right the first time. This is not always the case, and maybe a repair must be repeated a couple of times before the component works reliably again. The First Time Fix Rate is an important quality indicator and can be ascertained through the CMMS. Frequent temporary fixes are an example of not doing things right. Instead of investing effort in implementing a permanent solution, people often go for 'cheap and dirty' quick fixes. Such an attitude is highly detrimental for the system reliability and produces unnecessary additional costs.

Work safety is a mandatory element of service and falls into both areas, organizational efficiency and operational effectiveness. It requires comprehensive education of people and thorough control. Work safety requirements need to be properly addressed also in the description of maintenance activities. Apart from being their moral obligation of ensuring the safety of their people, project and business managers must also be aware of their personal legal responsibility in this regard. If work accidents happen as a result of formal deficiencies regarding work safety, the responsible persons, such as the project manager, the maintenance engineer, or the team leaders, may be subject to legal prosecution. Some examples for such formal deficiencies are: missing specific hazard profiles in job descriptions, missing specific system-related hazard profiles, missing or incomplete work-safety training, and lack of control regarding the compliance with the prescribed working and resting hours.

Continuous Improvement

Continuous improvement is an essential element of business culture and defines the special attitude or spirit of people to strive for changing things to the better. Different form business revolution which is a privilege of visionary people only, continuous improvement is available to everybody. The only things it requires are common sense and motivation. People should be sensitized by their managers to actively reflect about possible improvements they can make in their area of professional activity. Such improvements can be of technical nature, for example making a component more robust or eliminating a cause of repetitive failures. Improvements can also be made at operational level, like by adapting and enhancing maintenance plans. Without a basic level of organizational efficiency and of operational effectiveness, continuous improvement cannot work. As an example, if the effectiveness of the current practices is not regularly monitored and thus cannot be evaluated (as it would be the case in the absence of a CMMS or a maintenance engineer), it is impossible to improve maintenance plans.

Latest with any contract extension, customers expect to participate from productivity improvements and will ask for price reductions. Thus, service organizations incapable of permanently improving their performance will not be able to maintain their contract base. Service people should understand that continuous improvement is an important lever also for ensuring the long-term security of their own jobs.

Contract Development

Beside their regular operational duties, contract development is another important task of project managers. The most common aspect of contract development is scope extension, such as by servicing additional equipment. Another aspect is contract transformation, for instance conveying a lump-sum contract into a performance based one by introducing performance incentives. Acquiring and carrying out additional works, like design-out maintenance, modernization, upgrades, and small system modifications and expansions is another important project management task. Because these works are usually of lower complexity, they can be carried out to a large extent by the on-site service teams. Acquiring additional works does not only help to increase revenues but also enhances the personnel utilization, thus it is also improving the contract profitability.

Quite often, systems are operated over a longer period of time at higher performance levels than initially planned. This may be, for instance, the result of an incorrect initial assessment by the customer regarding the long-term requirements of his business. Because higher system utilization generally leads to more wear and tear and thus to an increased service effort, service contracts should be adapted accordingly. Such an adaptation should not only reflect the higher costs for the additional service and spare parts but also the fact that certain technical performance requirements, like the system reliability or availability, may be harder to achieve. Therefore, additionally to the contract price, the contractually agreed performance indicators as well as the handling of issues regarding the supplier's liability also need to be revised. Reacting to such situations and actively approaching the customers to address required contract amendments also falls into the responsibility of service project managers.

Most business managers fail in recognizing the tremendous potential of contract development. Instead of adding contract development to the business goals of their project managers, they often only stick to conventional targets like budget compliance. The potential of additional business in most large on-site service projects is estimated at approximately 5% of the basic annual service fee.

Generally, business managers do not spend enough time and effort for supporting their project managers. The latter are often left alone with their projects, and as long as everything works according to plan, business managers usually do not interfere. The less they hear from their projects, the happier they are.

Organization

Generally, for an installations company service can be set up as a vertical or as a functional organization. Which of these two solutions is better is a strongly debated question. My clear preference is the first one.

Setting up service as a vertical organization—as a separate business line alongside installations—is a clear indication that the company has a strong life-cycle oriented business approach and assigns service the same relevance as to the installations business divisions. Such a set-up is better suited for defining clear service goals, for developing a consistent service strategy, and for assigning unequivocal business responsibilities.

In a functional set-up, service is implemented as a horizontal layer underneath installations and is reported as part of the individual installations business lines. In such an organizational context, the risk that service will be treated as an inferior business and will always remain a second priority is high. Also, responsibility is much harder to assign: Who is ultimately responsible for the service results—the individual systems business lines or the service manager?

As a project business, an installations company requires a central organization and several project ones. The central organization is permanent, whereas the project ones are mobilized at start of a particular project and demobilized when the project ends. This is valid for the systems side and also for service.
The central service organization, usually located at the company's headquarters, is responsible for the following main tasks:

- Service strategy and business development
  - Strategy definition and implementation
  - Strategy alignment with the systems business lines (integrated service suppliers)
  - Identifying and selecting service opportunities (e.g. in the competitors' base)
  - Development and roll-out of new service offerings
  - Identifying modernization opportunities

- Planning, controlling and reporting
  - Conveying business targets into a business plan
  - Breaking down business targets to regional level
  - Aggregation of regional/project business information
  - Risk and opportunity management
  - Performance analysis

- Project release
  - Providing head office approval for new business opportunities according to their complexity and risk exposure

- Sales
  - Preparation of service bids
  - Negotiation
  - Alignment of sales activities with the systems business lines

- Continuous improvement
  - Collecting and sharing of best practices between regions and projects
  - Benchmarking

- ➔ Resource management
  - ◆ Pooling of personnel resources and exchange between projects and regions
  - ◆ Allocation of personal resources for new projects
  - ◆ Taking over of personnel from installation projects

- ➔ Service engineering and innovation
  - ◆ Development of maintenance plans
  - ◆ Defining standards, e.g. for maintenance management systems and condition monitoring
  - ◆ Collecting and analyzing project data

- ➔ Support
  - ◆ Central hotline
  - ◆ Central spare parts management department
  - ◆ Mobilization support

- ➔ Customer relationship management
  - ◆ Customer satisfaction review process
  - ◆ Site visits and customer interviews

In an international business, large sites with many projects may have their own permanent organization in charge of above-mentioned tasks. In this case, it is especially important to define clear responsibilities and to avoid redundancies with the head office and also between sites.

Two functions deserve special attention: Business Development and Mobilization Support.

Mature sites can develop their local business and mobilize new projects independently, while requiring little central support. Developing the service business in a new region—for instance by following a new installation or by addressing an attractive brown-field opportunity—requires intensive head-office support. In this regard, setting up a Regional Management structure and a Mobilization Team concept is a good solution.

Regional Managers are in charge of the business development in a particular region. This function requires individuals with a strong entrepreneurial, social, international, and subject-matter profile. For new sites, they identify business opportunities, manage the sales process, and organize the mobilization of new projects. For mature sites, they function as a link between the local organization and the head office and provide support whenever needed.

The mobilization is the most critical phase in the life cycle of a new project. During this phase, the project organization needs to be ramped up, the infrastructure needs to be installed, and the systems and processes need to be implemented. For accomplishing these tasks in a (usually) short period of time, a strong mobilization team is required. Such a team could be set up as a fix one located in the head office or in one of the larger sites. It could also be virtual, and as such ramped up on demand with resources from the head office and from other projects.

Supplier Maturity

In the systems and installations business, the maturity of service providers is measured by the quality of their services and by the degree of their ability to offer customers the integral asset management of their systems and installations throughout the entire life cycle. Mature service companies need to fulfill the following four requirements: (1) Demonstrate operational excellence; (2) constantly improve their performance; (3) develop an excellent understanding about the operational requirements of the serviced systems and adapt their services accordingly, and finally; (4) ensure the long-term sustainability of the serviced systems, in other words, protect their customers' investment. On the basis of these competences, mature service companies offer their customers a comprehensive portfolio of services including O&M, technical operation, and modernization.

Operational excellence and continuous improvement are closely linked with each other. Operational excellence is not static; it requires continuous improvement to be sustained. The good understanding of the operational requirements of systems and the ability to keep these systems up to date throughout their entire life cycle also depend on each other. Suppliers who understand their customers' business know how well the systems are suited for fulfilling the operational requirements. On this basis, they can propose their customers high value system improvement measures such as modernization, upgrading, and expansions.

A good indication that a service supplier embraces operational excellence is provided by the following aspects (not a complete list):

- The availability of comprehensive mobilization plans and the availability of a mobilization team for setting up new service projects
- The use of state-of-the-art CMMS and the availability of maintenance plans for all relevant system components
- The availability of SOPs for all relevant operational situations
- Expertise in advanced maintenance methods, including predictive maintenance, condition monitoring, root cause analysis and design-out maintenance
- An exact knowledge of the spare parts requirements and spare parts consumption of the system during operation (especially relevant for integrated service suppliers)
- A well-established Environmental Health and Safety Management System (EHSM)
- The availability of job descriptions for all relevant positions
- The availability of a formalized procedure for assessing the customer satisfaction

Operational excellence is the indispensable basis on which all other elements can build. It is the core of a supplier's '*maturity sphere*', while continuous improvement, operational understanding, and sustainability form the outer layers.
For many service companies, the last two elements are completely missing. Generic service providers generally do not have these elements in their strategic focus. Many integrated service suppliers also fail at recognizing their outstanding importance. These two maturity elements—operational understanding and the ability to offer sustainability solutions—differentiate simple service providers from genuine life-cycle partners of their customers. Suppliers who demonstrate operational excellence, understand the system requirements and the business goals of

their customers, and who are capable of offering sustainability solutions often maintain their service contracts over decades. In the service business for airport logistic systems, a couple of major hub airports around the world continue working with the same supplier for more than twenty years now. Sharing productivity gains (supplier) and providing an incentive for good results (customer) are a solid foundation for such a long-term win-win partnership.

Customers who are operating large, complex, and critical systems generally pursue the following two main goals: (1) maximizing the capitalization on the operational capabilities of their systems—this requires highest possible system reliability and lowest possible downtime; and (2) protecting their investment long-term—this requires preserving the systems in good technical condition, keeping them up to date, and continuously adapting them to changing operational requirements.
With regard to both of these goals, selecting a mature service provider as a genuine life-cycle partner has mission-critical relevance.

International Business

What makes managing an international service business for large installations especially challenging is that all aspects mentioned in the previous sections need to be interpreted individually at project level in the local context of the specific location where the service is executed.

Many aspects of this business differ significantly from one geographic region and even from one country to another. The most obvious differences are related to the local law, the local work culture, and local labor market.

From a legal perspective, contract and labor law are the most relevant elements.
With regard to contract law, it is especially important to understand how the contractor's liability is construed in the local market. The relevance of liquidated damages, penalties, direct and consequential damages and how these terms are applied in practice have to be taken into consideration during offer preparation, contract negotiation, as well as later during contract execution.
Local labor law also has a substantial influence on the suppliers' flexibility for ramping up or ramping down the organization as needed. It also plays an important role with regard to the personnel-related terminal risk at the end of contracts.

The local labor market is another important business parameter. Are there enough people with the required level of expertise locally available, or must these people be brought over form other regions? In the latter case, procuring visas and work permits can become a difficult undertaking. Another relevant aspect is the stability of the local labor market. If other important projects are pending in the region, such as large infrastructure ones, it can be expected that the labor market will tighten up and labor costs will increase. In such a market situation, the raiding of good people by competitors or other companies is a common phenomenon, and service managers need to be prepared to defend such attacks.

Depending on the specific legal regulations and labor market conditions in the region, the appropriate organizational setup needs to be individually defined for each project. In some countries, labor law is quite restrictive with regard to terminating people, like it could be required at the end of a project. Under such market conditions, the subcontracting of larger work packages to third parties could be a good solution, even though it usually increases costs. In regions where skilled labor is scarce, ramping up own resources would probably be the better tactic. Working in some regions could possibly require managing people with different cultural backgrounds. This does not go by itself and requires managers with intercultural experience.

Work productivity is also varying across regions and countries. The number of people or working hours needed for completing a job strongly depends on the maturity of the local labor market. Productivity is not only related to the level of professional education of people but is also a matter of personal work attitude. These parameters have to be taken into account already during offer preparation. Obviously, they also play an important role in the organizational ramp-up during project mobilization and later during project execution.

The personal motivation of people is a decisive factor. People who understand the relevance of their job for the success of their own business and also for the success of their customers work harder and pay more attention to the quality of their work. Different people find different things motivating. Money alone is not a good long-term motivator. Any salary raise loses its motivating effect after some time, and people expect a next increase. On the other hand, bad pay is a strong demotivator. Therefore, fair remuneration is a must. Additionally to receiving a fair pay, people must have the chance for developing their careers. If an unskilled worker gets the opportunity to train on the job and possibly the chance of receiving an internal qualification certificate, such a career step can be extremely motivating. In certain cultures, receiving exposure in the organization for good work results gives people an extra push. For example, issuing a monthly project bulletin is a good measure for aligning people. By informing about the project performance and about the customer's business and by also acknowledging individual and global accomplishments, such bulletins motivate people, foster their identification with the customer's business, and strengthen the community.

It is of great importance that project managers are fully accustomed with the local conditions. Assigning a person without this knowledge to manage a project could end in a disaster, even though this person possibly was successful somewhere else. Whether the manager should be a local person or an expat depends a lot on the local business culture and needs to be individually evaluated for each project.

In the international service business, success is largely determined by finding the right balance between central guidance and control on one side and self-government of the operational sites on the other. Giving the operational sites as much freedom as possible and allowing them to manage their local business autonomously usually leads to better global results. Residential service is a local business and cannot be managed from a central head office. Managers in the head offices of international service companies often make the mistake of trying to keep their subsidiaries at a too short leash. Instead of fostering the entrepreneurial spirit in the regions, they often micromanage the local business. Successful service companies put a lot of emphasis on developing strong managers for their regional subsidiaries who are capable of running their business independently and who can be trusted. Local managers should be given guidelines and targets and be left to manage their business according to their personal style and in accordance with the specific needs of the respective region. When they ask for support or advice, it must be given without delay. At the same time, it must be made clear that business responsibility cannot be socialized and must still remain with the local manager. The same applies for project managers, who should be capable of covering the complexity of large service projects. Finding good service project managers is quite difficult because most technical people still perceive service as an inferior and less challenging business as compared to engineering and installation. International service companies must pay more attention at identifying talented service people and at setting up an efficient system for their professional development. A large service project could be responsible for the asset management of a multi-hundred million Euro installation, could easily employ a couple of hundred service people, and manage a multi-million Euro annual budget. Thus, managers of such projects and managers of regional companies holding such projects must be true business people with entrepreneurial spirit and excellent qualifications in a large variety of areas.

Setting limits of authority for the regional companies is important. The engagement into projects with high criticality regarding technical content, contractual terms, customer related aspects, local law, or other market conditions should require formal head office approval. In this regard, systems and installations companies need to develop a standardized project approval process. This process should comprise a thorough risk and opportunity assessment as well as an escalation procedure defining the organizational level up to which a specific project must be escalated according to its criticality. The whole process must be based on standardized approval documents and must be binding for all transactions exceeding certain criticality thresholds. Before sending out an important binding offer, the project must be released in a formal approval meeting with participation of the responsible head-office service manager, the local service manager, and the local project manager if the latter is already available. Additionally, the participation of technical, legal, human resources, and supply chain experts may also be required. Such a procedure prevents that local businesses possibly engage into transactions exceeding their capabilities or bearing unacceptable risks. The approval process should be flexible enough to also take into account the maturity of regional companies. Subsidiaries with a good business track-record should be given more freedom to decide about the projects they want to acquire. Setting up a maturity matrix in which each regional unit receives a maturity score based on its business history would be a perfect instrument in this regard. Good managers will always try to enlarge their freedom of decision and thus will concentrate on constantly improving their maturity score. Therefore, they will avoid making mistakes and will try to deliver the best possible results.

Part of this project release process should also be a clarification regarding the segregation of responsibility between the head office and the regional units. It could be the case that for a new region, the head office is responsible for a first project until the local unit can build the required expertise for taking over. It is of utmost importance that head offices grant their support for a project as defined in the project release process and do not leave their regional subsidiaries alone.

The most critical phase of large resident service projects is the mobilization. At the end of this relatively short period of time, the organization has to be ramped-up, all processes have to be implemented, and all systems, for instance the CMMS, must be in function. For this important project step, service companies with an international footprint should set up a mobilization team. This could be a fix team made up of experts solely dedicated at mobilizing service projects and located in the service head office or in one of the main international sites. Alternatively, the mobilization team could also be virtual, in which experts from running contracts are gathered per case as needed. For large businesses, a fix team makes more sense because there are enough projects to work on, and thus there is no risk of under-utilization. The team members could also fulfill other tasks, such as business development, proposal work, and project support.

The following factors are of proven relevance for the success of an international service business:

- A lean head office, dedicated at supporting the regional sites in developing their own business.

  Different than in many other businesses, in service, value creation is entirely local. Therefore, one very important headquarters objective must be to foster the operational sites and to support them in managing their local business successfully. Such central support could be important, for instance, during the negotiation of large contacts or during the mobilization of large projects. Rather than micromanaging them, head offices have to be acting like coaches of their regional units. Though, many head offices fail in developing this understanding. Often, head office employees meet their counterparts in the regional units with arrogance and hubris. They perceive their own role as a given privilege, without caring too much about their real value contribution to the regional businesses. The role of many head office people is limited to communicating business targets and to collecting regional data for reporting purposes. This is often the result of not having the required subject matter expertise. Head office employees in charge of managing an international service business should be outstanding professionals with a strong operational background and exceptional communication and social skills. Such a professional profile is especially relevant in the area of business development. Head office employees must meet their regional counterparts at eye level and with respect. They must share the understanding that their success in their individual roles depends directly on the success of the regional businesses. The spirit of cooperation and trust must rule any relationship between head offices and their regional subsidiaries. The level of trust between the two is a good indicator for the maturity of an international service business.

- A good cooperation between the regional sites with regard to knowledge transfer and exchange of resources.

Not all regional units have the same level of expertise or the same amount of resources at their disposal. Therefore, it is essential that stronger units help weaker ones. Especially new subsidiaries are often overwhelmed by the complexity of negotiating an important service contract or of mobilizing a large service project and need support. Often, such support is concentrated only in the head office. Managers of international businesses must bear in mind that keeping too many personnel resources centrally may result in under-utilization and also has the downside that people may gradually lose their operational touch. Therefore, organizing support from other regions, like by setting up a virtual mobilization team composed of experts from other operational sites, has many advantages. People having a direct operational background will always be looking for solutions of high practical feasibility. Working in other regions and using their knowledge for helping their colleagues in setting up their own business gives people professional satisfaction and a strong sense of purpose. It is the head office managers' job to implement such a culture of collaboration.

By adhering to these two principles, successful service suppliers have established a strong autonomous regional business generating the vast majority of the company's service revenues.

Technology and Innovation

Many new technological developments are also relevant for service, like in the area of new sensors, data acquisition and analysis, and artificial intelligence. By introducing the latest innovations, for example in the field of condition monitoring, predictive maintenance, advanced operational data analysis, and decision support, service can benefit a lot. A tendency resulting from the general digitalization trend is to sometimes introduce such innovations just because they are available. Without a sound justification related to operational and equipment requirements and with no measurable financial outcome, such investments do not make sense. In the absence of such a justification, they are just gimmicks of no business value.

As a business, service must generate customer value and yield profits. Each innovation must follow the same rational. For example, a new condition monitoring application must save costs by reducing the amount of man-hours spent on inspections and unplanned repairs. The investment would only make economic sense if the corresponding service headcounts could either be used in other areas of activity or reduced accordingly. Alternatively, the new technology would have to increase the operational reliability of systems and thus reduce the customers' costs resulting from lost production. In this case, the investment would yield a benefit for the service provider only if the customer is willing to pay for this additional value or if it increases the supplier's chances for getting his contract renewed. Not all systems and installations are equally suited for the introduction of new technologies. For example, in industrial installations with large critical components, like motors, pumps, and blowers, which usually have a predictive failure pattern, condition monitoring (CM) makes a lot of sense. It can help to detect a potential failure in an early stage, enabling that a planned repair is carried out in due time for preventing that the system breaks down. As another example, remote diagnostics and predictive maintenance supported by advanced sensors and data analysis algorithms have substantially increased the operational reliability and safety of critical rolling stock such as high-speed trains. The severe failure consequences of such critical equipment justify the investment into advanced condition monitoring systems as well as the effort spent on monitoring and analyzing the produced data.

In the past, large distributed systems composed of many small components with a rather random failure pattern, such as airport baggage systems, were not suitable for CM. The costs for the installation of CM equipment would have been too high. New technologies such as the *motor current signature analysis* make condition monitoring applicable nowadays also for these systems. Modern drive systems provide motor current information even for lower power ratings and thus allow assessing the health of baggage conveyors without any additional investment in other CM technology such as vibration sensors. The advanced analysis of such data produces valuable information not only about the drive system itself but also about the attached mechanical equipment.

In some service organizations, substantial investments into new technologies are made over years without a measurable financial return from running projects. Naturally, new technologies must be tested and assessed for applicability. Live installations of customers are a good place for such tests. In

these cases, such endeavors have a pilot character, and an immediate financial return cannot be expected. Nevertheless, service managers must insist on a realistic return of such investments.
Assessing the business potential of new technologies and implementing only those solutions which increase the service efficiency and/or generate other values for which the customers are willing to pay is an important aspect of service innovation. Customers with critical systems will always prefer service suppliers who combine people excellence with the ability to make use of the latest technological innovations.

Because today everybody talks about digital transformation, many service managers make the mistake of expecting too much additional business related to the introduction of new technologies. Generic goals like "We need to generate 20% of our revenues from digital business," are often set without regard to their practical feasibility. Service companies which generate most of their business with O&M will have great difficulties in reaching such targets. Customers who have outsourced the integral service of their systems are reluctant to spend additional money for the introduction of advanced technologies. To the contrary, if the suppliers are able to save costs, for instance by implementing a new condition monitoring system, the customers will usually insist on sharing these gains by asking for a reduction of the service price—latest when the contract is due for renewal.

Large systems produce a huge amount of operational data. Analyzing this data and providing the customers with valuable decision support information is often a good opportunity for additional digital business, like in the following example from airport logistics:

In the airports, early bag stores are used as an intermediate storage for bags which have been checked-in early or are waiting for a connecting flight. By releasing these bags only short before the flight, congestion in the baggage system can be avoided. Usually, early bag stores are a critical resource for the baggage handling process. Thus, their utilization by the different airlines is an important information for the airport operators. The airport fees for the airlines could be individually adapted according to their utilization of resources.

'Fitness for service' is an increasingly important quality parameter of new systems and installations and must be in the main focus of the R&D departments of the systems units. For example, the use of drives which produce useful diagnostic data, such as the current signature, in combination with an automated data storage and retrieval mechanism in the IT system of the installation makes a lot of sense from a TCO perspective. In the life-cycle cost balance of a critical system, the savings resulting from increased service efficiency and from avoided system downtime generally offset the extra initial expenditures by far. Furthermore, 'fitness for service' can provide an important competitive edge and the decisive argument for winning a new installations contracts.

In conclusion, the introduction of new technologies in service must always follow an economic rationale and should not be the result of just wanting to follow a trend.

There is a risk that by increasing their focus on new technologies, service companies forget about the decisive role motivated and knowledgeable people still play for the success of their business.

The Value of Service

Contrary to physical technical assets, the service associated with keeping these items in good shape is immaterial, and therefore its value is harder to define. Customers usually know precisely how much they want to spend for a product or an installation. On the other hand, the only thing they often know about the pertaining service is that they want to spend as little as possible for it.

This chapter addresses customers who intend to outsource the service for their systems, with the aim of supporting them in the selection process of the appropriate service provider. It also addresses service companies to help them substantiate the value of their offerings. As the goals of service are always the same, most aspects addressed in this chapter are also of interest for the in-house service departments of customers.

Everybody knows that it is impossible to operate a complex technical asset, like a large airport baggage handling system or an industrial production line, without any service. But how to determine the value of good service and how to differentiate good service from poor service—in terms of price and quality?

For answering these questions, the starting point would be to think about the goals of service. Service must:

(1) ensure the safe and reliable operation of the installation;

(2) preserve the installation in good technical condition, thus protect the customer's initial investment;

(3) adapt the installation to changing operational and technical requirements through upgrading and modernization.

The easiest way for assessing the value of service is by evaluating the consequences of bad service according to the three above-mentioned service goals.

(1) The value of the reliable operation of an installation is mainly determined by the 'costs of lost production.' In a processing or manufacturing plant, these costs are determined by the amount of goods that cannot be produced because of a failure of the installation. Losses caused by a major failure of a production unit in the automotive industry, like an assembly line, can reach a couple of thousand Euros per minute. As another example, a major failure of the baggage handling system (BHS) in a large airport may cause that 10,000 bags are left behind and must be reprocessed and rejoined with the passenger at a later time. A conservative estimation of these costs is 100 Euros per 'left behind bag.' Furthermore, the airport may be subject to penalties toward the airlines for contract non-fulfillment. Thus, the damage caused by such an incident could easily achieve the magnitude of millions.

In many applications, the unreliable function of an installation also exposes the operator to incalculable risks regarding the work and environmental safety. Additionally to these losses, the immaterial damage, for example the loss of reputation, must also be taken into consideration.

(2) A large installation represents a significant investment and should function reliably over its intended life. Due to poor service, some installations do not reach their intended end of life, and therefore a part of the investment is wasted. After a couple

of years, some installations are in such a poor technical condition that they need a major overhaul to continue operating.

(3) Even though all regular maintenance tasks are carried out with all required diligence, the reliable operation of the system still may be jeopardized. Many parts may become obsolete and need to be replaced by modern ones. This is especially the case of controls and IT, where the original suppliers are drastically increasing the price for spare parts and support after a certain period of time or are terminating the support for older systems at all. The same also applies for many electro-mechanical components. It is the duty of service providers to observe such developments and to propose upgrading and modernization solutions for preserving the system in maintainable condition.
The operating conditions may also have changed since the initial installation and therefore demand an adaptation of the system to the new requirements. As an example, some parcel logistics installations are not capable of processing the tremendously increased volume of parcels resulting from the general trend toward online commerce. In many such cases, an upgrade or modernization with newer and more advanced components not only preserves the integrity of the installation but also yields opportunities for a significant performance increase.

Each mature service provider should be able to address all the three above-mentioned goals. In the selection process of a service provider, customers should ask the following questions:

(1) "How do you make sure that my system works reliably, especially during the critical operation periods when downtime immediately leads to a substantial loss of production."

Many customers think that this issue can be solved by setting the focus on system availability only. This is too shortsighted. The installation may fail in a critical phase of operation and still perform above the required monthly availability level.

To this question, a smart answer would be:

"We have predictive measures in place which inform us early enough about the possible failure of critical components. Additionally, we have developed standard operating procedures for ensuring a swift system recovery after an (improbable) breakdown, with the aim of keeping the consequences of such failure as low as possible."

(2) "What is your strategy for preserving the good technical condition of my system, thus for making sure that it does not degrade over time and that it will perform stably over its entire intended life period."

Few customers have this important aspect on their radar screen and are assuming that by setting certain technical and operational targets, such as availability and reliability, the system will automatically stay in good condition.

At this point, quality service providers will answer:

"Additionally to carrying out all maintenance activities with all required care, we monitor the system condition as part of our annual asset condition review. A central part of this review is targeted at identifying all parts that may not be available any longer and at proposing upgrades and substitutions as needed."

(3) "Our system is quite old and may not fulfill future performance requirements. How can you support us in the decision process whether we should be investing into a new system or rather in extending the life of the existing one?"

Mature service providers should be able to answer:

"We have the adequate processes and technological expertise for assessing the technical feasibility and economical value of a potential system modernization with focus on life extension and performance increase."

Experience shows that a major obstacle for achieving above-mentioned goals is the frequent change of service suppliers. In such a case, and especially if in the selection of a new supplier the lowest possible price is the prevailing argument, suppliers will always follow the path of least effort: making some profit in the short term without much consideration for the life-cycle aspects of the installation. Knowing that the likelihood of losing the contract after a couple of years is quite high, why would suppliers be concerned about the long-term system condition? This is one of the reasons why many installations are in a deplorable technical condition already after two or three terms of poor service.
Many people are asking about the ROI of service. This question is difficult to answer because there is no alternative to servicing technical assets. Not servicing an installation comes equal to not brushing one's teeth. Latter would function well for a while even without brushing, but the long-term consequences would be painful and expensive.

Therefore, I will try to make some considerations on the ROI of service based on a comparison between two scenarios:

(1) selecting a low-cost provider with low technological profile

(2) selecting a mature provider with a comprehensive life-cycle approach

As a reference installation, I am picking a large airport baggage handling system (BHS) with an asset replacement value of 150 mil Euros. Such a system can be found in mid-size hub airports processing around 30 mil passengers, respectively around 30 mil bags per year (based on a bag/passenger ratio of 1). The regular life of such a system is around 30 to 40 years.

If the customer has outsourced the services, the first couple of service terms are usually executed by the company that has built the system. Because of the system complexity and the proprietary character of the IT and the controls, customers prefer to keep the manufacturer in the loop until the system proves to work stably. By the end of the second term (after 2x5 years = 10 years), customers may want to save costs by opening competition also to cheaper providers with a lower technological profile.

The maintenance factor[1] of a large BHS is around 3%. Thus, the annual costs of maintenance are around 4.5 mil Euros.
This value can be considered as a reference for Western Europe, but it may vary quite substantially across countries, depending mainly on the local labor costs. This number does not include costs associated with the technical operation of the installation, which is often also part of many large contracts.

---

[1] *maintenance factor = annual maintenance costs / asset replacement value*

Experience shows that in an open tender for the maintenance of a large BHS the prices offered by mature service providers, such as the service organization of the system manufacturer, may be around 15% higher than the offers of providers who enter competition mainly on the basis of low prices. Competitors with unacceptably low offers are usually disqualified.

Thus, by choosing the cheaper provider, the customer would be able to save 675 thousand Euros per year or, in other words, 3.4 mil Euros over a contract term of 5 years.

This is the positive side of such an approach.

In the following, I will try to assess the downside of this choice.

(1) Lost production

It can be assumed that even a well maintained and operated BHS system in a larger airport will experience *one major failure every 15 years*. Such an event is often caused by the failure of the IT and/or the controls system and usually results in a total stop of the entire installation.

Failures of other critical equipment such as sorters or high-speed transfer lines are usually less severe (redundant equipment is often available) but still can be very disturbing. If the system manufacturer is maintaining the installation and thus is already having people on site who understand the system, it can be further assumed that operation can be restored in less than one day. The service people will probably be able to locate the failure pretty soon and have standard recovery procedures in place for bringing the system back into operation in the shortest possible period of time. Additionally, they can also rely on the support of the system engineers in the development departments of their headquarters.

This is something generic providers cannot do. For just locating the failure, they usually have to involve the system supplier, and the whole recovery process would take significantly longer. In this case, the likelihood of such a failure to occur is higher (handling failures, faulty parametrization), and the restoration time is substantially longer. Therefore, if the system is maintained by a service provider with low technological profile, it can be assumed that such a catastrophic failure may occur *every 5 years*.

What does this mean in financial terms?

Losing one day of operation of such a large BHS means that theoretically approximately 80,000 bags cannot be processed. In practice, this value can be sometimes reduced by running the system in manual mode or by using manual labor for handling the bags. Therefore, if, as an assumption, the system is down for one day and one third of the bags may still be processed, 53,000 bags may still be left behind. This means that the majority of passengers will leave without their luggage. Using the already mentioned conservative estimation of costs per left bag of 100 Euros, the damage caused by such a major system failure would sum up to the impressive amount of 5.3 mil Euros.

Some customers may think that the service provider must compensate them for such losses. In most cases, this is an illusion. To be made responsible for such direct damages, the service provider must be in default. This is not necessarily the case, and if, such default is usually hard to prove. In this regard, reference is made to the *Contracts* chapter: *Supplier's Liability*.

Additionally, it must be taken into account that by not having the financial strength to absorb such losses, smaller suppliers without the adequate financial robustness would be driven into bankruptcy.

Therefore, either the airport or the airlines (depending on the specific terms of their contract) will have to bear such costs. As a consequence, the related annual risk exposure to be taken into account by the airport would be 5.3 mil / 15 = 353 thousand Euros in the case of a mature service provider as compared to 5.3 mil / 5 = 1 mil Euros for an immature one. Thus, in terms of lost production, the annual cost of poor service would be 650 thousand Euros. These numbers are rather conservative because they are based on major incidents only and do not take into account the lost production caused by less critical failures of electro-mechanical equipment such as sorters or transfer lines. If the system is not maintained well (poor preventive maintenance, temporary fixes, no predictive maintenance, stock-outs of critical parts), such failures will occur regularly and jeopardize the reliable operation of the installation.

(2) Technical system condition

Some customers change their service providers frequently, for example every 3 years, and the service is often carried out by suppliers with low technological profile. In such cases, the system condition will degrade rapidly, often down to the point where failures are occurring on a regular basis and the installation cannot fulfill its operational requirements any longer. In this situation, no solid supplier would accept to take over the service for such a system without carrying out an upfront major system overhaul. From experience, the technical condition of systems which are not maintained well degrades (excessive wear, temporary fixes, low-quality spare parts) by 3-5% annually. This means that already after three terms of 3 years each the technical degradation can reach 30%. Under these conditions, the system cannot work reliably any longer and needs a major overhaul. Not all parts are equally affected by wear and tear. For example, IT and controls hardware degrades mainly with time, and steel structures in an indoor environment are less sensitive to poor service. Well maintained systems are also affected by degradation and need an upgrading, but at a far slower pace. Assuming that in this case the degradation is half as fast, it would take twice as long for the system to degrade to the same extent.

For assessing the financial consequences of an accelerated system degradation caused by bad service, only one fifth of the asset value, consisting of moving parts, motors, gearboxes, pulleys, carts, rails and others, are considered relevant in this regard. This means that one fifth of the 150 mil Euro installation = technical assets worth 30 mil Euros will be degraded and will need an overhaul. Assuming that such a comprehensive overhaul would cost one third of the original asset value, 10 mil Euros need to be spent for restoring the full function of the installation. This would be the case after approximately 9 years of poor service, respectively after 18 years if the system was correctly maintained. With regard to the second goal of service—the preservation of the good technical condition of the installation—the costs for the airport as a consequence of bad service would be around 0.5 mil Euros per year. These numbers do not include the costs of upgrades for IT and controls, which will be considered in the next topic.

(3) Modernization and upgrading

As mentioned before, IT and control systems degrade with time. Even though these systems do not wear out, they have a limited life. After a certain period of time, the original manufacturers stop supporting older systems and/or are drastically increasing the price for spare parts and service. For maintaining the reliable function of the installation, upgrades and modernization of these systems are indispensable. For estimating the financial impact of this aspect, a couple of assumptions need to be made: (1) IT systems reach their end of life after 7 years and control systems after 15 to 20 years. (2) The costs for the upgrade of these two systems pertaining to the BHS of an airport as specified in the beginning are around 5 mil Euros for the IT and 8 mil Euros for the controls. Thus, over 20 years the total costs for upgrading and modernizing the IT and the control systems sum up to (3x5) + (1x8) = 23 mil Euros. This equals to more than 1 mil Euros per year. The duration of each of these projects is about one year. As the airport cannot be stopped over a longer period of time, these works need to be executed dynamically during regular operation of the system. This aspect makes these projects highly complex and critical. Usually, the systems can be made available only in periods with low traffic, and after each project step the function of the installation must be fully restored.

Because these projects can normally be executed only by the original supplier, it is obviously very advantageous to have the same company also responsible for the service of the installation: (1) there are a lot of synergies between the on-site service team and the project organization, e.g. service technicians, who are on site anyway, can execute many of these works; (2) the co-ordination between project and service is far better, e. g the restoration of the function of the system after a project step is usually significantly faster; (3) the total responsibility is clearly defined and cross-blaming is not possible. Keeping these aspects in mind, it can be assumed that modernization and upgrading projects can be executed at *30% less in terms of costs* and *20% less in terms of duration*. Over 20 years of BHS operation, this represents total savings of almost 7 mil Euros (350 thousand per year) in terms of costs and of around 10 months in terms of project duration (half a month or 15 days per year) if the original supplier is also responsible for the service of the installation. While the magnitude of cost savings is obvious, the monetary value of a reduced project duration is harder to evaluate. It can be assumed that 10% of the reduction in project duration translates directly into higher availability of the system to operate during regular operation hours; this equals to additional 36 annual hours (15 x 24h x 10%) of (peak-hour) operation, when the system is needed most. Airports can calculate the monetary value of this additional system availability on the basis of their specific operational and financial parameters.

The conclusion which can be drawn on the basis of these findings is obvious:

Blindly saving on service translates into much higher costs over the entire life cycle of an installation.

In the example of the BHS in a larger airport, the losses caused by bad service would be more than double higher than the savings realized by employing a cheap and immature service provider.

Years		1	2	3	4	5	Total
Savings [k€]	Service	**675**	**675**	**675**	**675**	**675**	**3,375**
Costs [k€]	Lost Production	650	650	650	650	650	3,250
	System Condition	500	500	500	500	500	2,500
	Upgrading	350	350	350	350	350	1,750
	Total Costs	**1,500**	**1,500**	**1,500**	**1,500**	**1,500**	**7,500**

Even though installations differ significantly across different industries, above reasoning applies for the majority of technical systems of large size and high complexity. The numbers may differ, but the essence of the message remains unchanged:

Cheap service never pays off in long term.

This does not mean that customers should not care about the service fees they pay to their suppliers. To the contrary, they need to develop an understanding about how these costs are built and challenge their suppliers of choice accordingly. They must make clear that they do not allow their suppliers to abuse a dominant market position, such as resulting from proprietary systems. To the benefit of both parties, customers and suppliers should join efforts toward forging a long-term partnership based on fairness and trust. Fairness, for instance, means sharing the benefits stemming from continuous improvement.

One of the obstacles in the process of building such a trustful long-term relationship lies in the fact that usually the purchasing departments of the customers have the dominant role in the (re-)negotiation of such contracts. It is often the case that operational people of the customers are completely missing from these meetings. This often leads to a situation when customers and suppliers perceive themselves more as opponents rather than partners, and thus a win-win relationship cannot be established. In many cases, the tender conditions for new service contracts specify that automatically the lowest bid will win. Even though only pre-qualified suppliers are admitted for submitting offers, this kind of procedure completely ignores the value of good service by reducing it to its price. As a consequence, many customers suffer from poor service and are not able to fully capitalize on the potential of their technical assets.

Customers need to develop a life-cycle strategy for their installations. This includes identifying the critical equipment, assessing the damage potential of equipment failure (like the monetary value of lost production), and defining how the technical condition and the long-term operational capability should be preserved over the entire life of the installation. On the basis of this strategy, they should select a service provider capable of addressing all of these aspects.

Business Valuation

The purpose of this chapter is to provide some guidance regarding the methodology used in the valuation process of service companies and to point out some special aspects that have to be taken into consideration in this matter.

Valuating a service business is of relevance in the following cases:

(1) In the process of acquiring an installations company comprising its systems and also its service business

In such a case, both sides of the business need to be valued. It is important to observe that the parameters going into the valuation of a systems business as compared to a service business differ significantly. Obviously, it only makes sense to acquire both businesses, and buying one without the other would destroy value. The service business of an installations company can only grow if it is continuously funneled with new service opportunities resulting from the company's new installations. On the other side, without service an installation company would lose approximately one third of its business potential.

(2) In the process of acquiring a generic service company

As mentioned before, such an acquisition for the mere purpose of boosting sales figures generally does not make sense, for the following reason: The genuine value of a generic service company lies mainly in the present value of its running contracts. In most cases, generic service providers are servicing installations of small and middle complexity, and their prevailing value proposition are lower prices. In this kind of business, competition is intense. Therefore, the danger of being substituted by another supplier at the end of the running term is high. In theory, all of these contracts could be acquired after expiration at no costs. So, why pay for them?

The acquisition of a generic service provider should always be driven by a higher strategic goal, such as establishing a business bridgehead in a new market or gaining access to strategic customers.

In the following, two valuation scenarios will be discussed:

- The valuation of the service business of a mature installations company (integrated service supplier)
- The valuation of a mature generic service provider

The following aspects apply in both cases:

Service generally requires comparatively little assets. Therefore, in many cases (and also in the examples that are presented in this chapter) assets can be neglected in the valuation. For simplicity, it will be further assumed that the business has no debt. The valuations presented in the following are thus made on a net asset, net cash, and net debt basis. By acquiring a service company, the buyer is usually interested in the business's **equity,** which means that he will take over also all liabilities, and in gaining the **controlling interest** over the business.
Because in this case the main focus is on the prospective long-term development of the business, the valuation is made on the

basis of a **going concern**, meaning that the business will not be liquidated and thus will continue to exist forever.
It will be further assumed that also all other liabilities can be neglected, which means that the fair market value (FMV) of the company is equal to the value of its equity.
Service contracts usually have a longer duration (3-5 years) and often include prolongation options. Thus, the development of the business for the first couple of years is quite clear, and the resulting cash flows for this initial period can be determined quite precisely. The long-term development is harder to predict. It is influenced by several factors, such as the general development of the market, the development of the systems business (for integrated service suppliers), the business strategy, and the competitive environment.

Based on the above-mentioned specific aspects of service and also because consistent information required for a comparative valuation approach (based on previous comparable transactions) does not exist, the most precise method for determining the market value of a service company is the Discounted Cash Flow (DCF) valuation.

Determining a company's market value with the DCF method requires calculating the following two components:

- The present value (PV) of the free cash flows (FCF) over an initial period. This initial period needs to be defined individually for each target depending on the structure of its service contracts.

- The present value of the company's terminal value (TV) at the end of the above-mentioned initial period.

Valuation of an integrated service supplier

The valuation of the service business of an installations company (integrated service supplier) will be demonstrated by means of a hypothetical example based on the following assumptions:

➔ Mature company, well established in the market, with a proven positive track record in both fields, systems and service

For such a company, and especially for the service part, it can be assumed that the development over the last couple of years can be extrapolated quite well into the future. Thus, the company's future business performance can be estimated quite accurately, and the consistency of the company's development plans (as presented by the seller) can be assessed quite easily. Because in service the majority of the business is stemming from the contract base (older contracts which are regularly renewed), not losing any of these contracts is mission critical. Retaining and renewing running contracts is the most important success factor in the service business. Therefore, excellent customer relationship management (CRM) is especially important in this trade. A well-established customer satisfaction review process is mandatory in this regard.

➔ Outsourcing friendly market

For the service business, operating in an outsourcing friendly (high outsourcing maturity) environment is an assurance that the majority of the company's future installations will translate into service business opportunities. It thus can be assumed that the majority of running service contracts will be renewed (if the customers are satisfied with the performance of their service provider).

➔ Good business mix between systems and service (75% systems and 25% service)

In the case of mature installations companies operating in an outsourcing friendly environment, a share of the service business of greater than 25% indicates that the company has a consistent life-cycle approach. Thus, if the installations business is strong, it can be assumed that the company will systematically capitalize on all service opportunities yielded by its new installations, and therefore the service business will grow.

The service portfolio is also of great importance. For mature service companies operating in an outsourcing friendly market, integral O&M should be the main element, with a share of around 70% or more. A strong modernization business is a further indication for a consistent life-cycle orientation. Successful integrated service suppliers generate 15% or more of their business from upgrading and modernization projects.

For the business valuation according to the DCF method, two parameters are of special relevance:

(1) The *initial period* (number of years) used for calculating the business's present value on the basis of its future FCF ($PV_{(FCF)}$).

This period must be selected in a way that minimum 80% of the future business can be substantiated by known contracts. The majority of this business is stemming from running contracts and contracts with high chances for renewal or extension. In this regard, contracts that have already been renewed in the past and/or pertain to large and complex systems with many proprietary elements are the most relevant. Additionally, the planning for this initial period should also consider the service opportunities yielded by new own installations going live in the next future.

Under the assumption that the majority of the business is generated by a couple of large O&M contracts, the period used for calculating the $PV_{(FCF)}$ should be selected between 1.5 and 2 times the average duration of these contracts. If the average duration of large contracts is (for example) 5 years, this initial period should be selected between 7 to 10 years.
In the example presented in Table 1, the initial period used for the calculation of the $PV_{(FCF)}$ is 10 years.

(2) The outer years *(perpetual) business growth rate* which is used for calculating the company's terminal value.

As mentioned before, service is a cumulative business. If running contracts (and especially the large ones) are regularly renewed, the company can build a substantial contract base. The growth is generated by new contracts, which in the case of integrated service suppliers will stem mainly from their own new installations going into operation. Thus, the main driver for service growth are successful new installations which in turn generate new service opportunities. Because in the case of a mature company the base of running service contracts is significantly larger than the additional annual service business resulting from own new installations, the growth rate of service is rather moderate, and thus service can generally be considered a *slow-growth business*. One the other hand, the large service contract base is an insurance that even in periods with a low volume of new installations the running contracts will continue to generate solid revenues. Thus, service can be also considered a *low-risk business*, at least compared to the installations one. These facts need to be taken into account for defining the *risk premium* in the *risk-adjusted discount rate* used for calculating present values and also for selecting the appropriate *perpetual growth rate.* Latter should be selected significantly lower than the average growth rate of the business during the *initial period*.

Calculating the present value of a business on the basis of its generated future cash flows requires selecting an appropriate discount rate. In this regard, the seller as well as the buyer of the business would probably use their individual *weighted average of capital cos*t (WACC). With a different mix between equity and debt in the capital structure, the individual WACC of seller and buyer would probably vary. Thus, the present values of the business as calculated by the two parties would also deviate from each other.
For determining a more "objective" business value, I therefore recommend using a *risk-adjusted discount rate* which takes into consideration the general and the specific risks of the particular business. Each of these risks determines a *risk premium* which has to be added on top of the long-term risk-free rate.

Which are such risks that could apply for the integrated service business of an installations company?

The following risks are typical and should always be assessed and applied:

➔ The *operational risk* that service projects may not yield the expected financial performance. Such risks could be resulting for example from having to use more personnel and spare parts than originally planned. They could also be the result of increasing labor costs due to a shortage of skilled people in the local market. Further risk elements could be excessive repairs, an unstable installation or uncooperative customers.
For mature integrated service suppliers, my recommendation for this risk premium is 1% to 2%. In the example, it is 1.0%.

➔ The *contractual risk* resulting from the non-fulfillment of contractual obligations. These could be liquidated damages for not reaching certain performance indicators or (direct and consequential) damages as a result of the supplier's default.
For mature suppliers, this risk premium should be selected between 0,5% and 1.5%. In the example, it is 1.0%.

➔ The *orders risk* reflecting that new service projects cannot be acquired as planned. This could be the result of the fact that the installations business may not be capable of selling enough new installations which can turn into service opportunities. It could also be the result of not being capable of capturing important new service contracts (for example because customers may decide to insource the service). Or it could also reflect the fact that the company may not be able to renew important running service contracts.
This risk premium could be set at one third of the average service business growth rate. In the example, the

orders risk is 1.5%.

➔ The *business transfer risk* reflecting a couple of typical uncertainties associated with the change of ownership of a business. Once the information about such a potential change reaches the market, competitors usually take advantage of the uncertainty among the company employees by trying to take over the best people. Will the company lose key experts and managers during this process? To which extent will this affect the performance? Will proprietary information leak to competitors? Will the workforce support the change or will it rather try to impair it? How will the customers react? Will they accept that their service contracts will be transferred to another party? Unknown project risks and business liabilities are a further element of uncertainty. Generally, sellers are emphasizing opportunities while trying to obscure risks. How transparent in this regard is the information presented by the seller?
These are a couple of questions which need to be answered for assessing these risks. For the acquisition of a mature business, this is the most incalculable and therefore greatest risk. In this example, the business transfer risk is evaluated at 4.0%

➔ The *inflation risk* should have the same value as used in the FCF calculation. In this example, it is 2.0%.

Regarding the operational and contractual risks, some readers may argue that these risks are already included in the calculation of contracts and thus should not be applied for a second time at this point. If contracts always perform as planned, if risk accruals at project level are always sufficient and can even be converted into additional profit at the end of projects, and if 'bad projects' never occur, then the above observation is valid. But such businesses exist only in theory. The values for these risks used in this example are quite low, reflecting the fact that we talk about a mature company with a positive business track record.

The above-identified individual risks sum up to a risk premium of 9.5% which needs to be added on top of the risk-free interest rate, in this example 3%. Thus, the discount rate would be 12.5%.

Obviously, the selling company will present its own business planning regarding the mid-term development of service sales and profit. Nevertheless, it is recommended to prove in the due diligence process that that these figures are justified by also analyzing the development of the installations business. In this example, it will be assumed that the installations business is a slow growing business, growing at 2.5% per year. A further assumption is that the only source of service growth are the own new installations of the company. For calculating the additional service business resulting from these new installations, two more parameters need to be defined: The *maintenance factor [%]* (the value of the potential annual service business resulting from an installation, divided by the value of this installation) and the *service capture rate [%]* (how much of the service potential yielded by the installations business turns into real service). Installation sales do not immediately trigger service sales. Only after the installation project is finished and the system goes into operation, service can start. In this example, it will be assumed that the average duration of installation projects is two years. Therefore, the service potential in one year is calculated based on the installations volume from two years before. It is further important to keep in mind that the base of running projects is subject to a certain *erosion* triggered by various factors: Some service projects may not be renewed. The scope of certain service projects may be reduced due to the insourcing of activities by the customers. The service fees will be reduced over time due to productivity gains which need to be shared with the customers.

Because service is a business generally not requiring significant assets, depreciation, capital expenditures and increases in net working capital can be neglected in the FCF calculation. Thus, the FCF is determined only by the EBIT and the tax rate.

The terminal value of the business is calculated on the basis of the FCF generated by the company in the year following the initial period used for calculating the company's $PV_{(FCF)}$. In the example, this would be year 11. At this point, the long-term sustainability of the business needs to be assessed. Therefore, a *sustainability factor (SF)* reflecting the long-term risks will be introduced in the terminal value calculation. In the case of an integrated service supplier, these long-term risks could be linked to:

➔ Stability of the installations business

- Will the market continue to grow, or will it run into saturation?
- How is the installations business positioned compared to its competitors, regarding its solutions and product portfolio, innovation, and project execution capabilities?

→ Long-term capability of converting new installations into service

- Will the share of large and complex systems with many proprietary components continue to by high?
- Does the company have a consistent service strategy, and is this strategy aligned with the installations business?
- Did the service supplier succeed in acquiring all non-captive service contracts for larger own installations (capture rate)?

→ Long-term capability of retaining running contracts

- Are there any changes expected regarding the general outsourcing maturity of the service market?
- Do large customers consider insourcing?
- Was the integrated service supplier capable of renewing the majority of his running contracts?
- How well is the service provider entrenched in the customers' business, for example by offering modernization solutions?
- How well established is the Customer Relationship Management (CRM)?

The following parameters are used for the valuation presented in Table 1.

Parameter		Value
Growth Rate Installations (GR)		2.5%
Maintenance Factor (MF)		3.0%
Capture Rate Service (CR)		70.0%
Erosion Rate Service (ER)		3.0%
Inflation Rate (IR)		2.0%
EBIT Service		12.0%
Discount Rate Service (DR)		12.5%
	Risk Free Invest 3.0%	
	Operational Risk Service 1.0%	
	Contractual Risk Service 1.0%	
	Orders Risk 1.5%	
	Business Transfer Risk 4.0%	
	Inflation 2.0%	
Perpetual Growth Rate Service (PGR)		1.0%
Terminal Value Sustainability Factor (SF)		70.0%
Tax Rate (TR)		25.0%

Year	-3	-2	-1	1	2	3	4	5	6	7	8	9	10	11
Installations [mil] @GR +2.5%	278	285	293	300	308	315	323	331	339	348	357	366	375	
Service Potential @MF 3.0%					8.8	9.0	9.2	9.5	9.7	9.9	10.2	10.4	10.7	
Captured Service @CR 70%					6.1	6.3	6.5	6.6	6.8	7.0	7.1	7.3	7.5	
Service Erosion @ER -3.0%					-3.0	-3.2	-3.3	-3.5	-3.6	-3.8	-4.0	-4.1	-4.3	
Service Inflation @IR 2.0%					2.0	2.1	2.2	2.3	2.4	2.5	2.6	2.8	2.9	
Service Sales	90	93	96	100	105	110	116	121	127	132	138	144	150	157
Service Growth Rate [%]					5.1	5.0	4.8	4.7	4.6	4.5	4.4	4.3	4.2	
Service EBIT @ EBIT 12.0%	11	11	12	12	13	13	14	15	15	16	17	17	18	19
Service FCF @TR 25%	8	8	9	**9**	**9**	**10**	**10**	**11**	**11**	**12**	**12**	**13**	**14**	**14**
				⇩	⇦	⇦	⇦	⇦	⇦	⇦	⇦	⇦	⇦	⇩
Present FCF Value @DR 12.5%		⇩	⇦	**59**										⇩
		⇩												⇩
Terminal Value @PGR 1.0%		⇩												**157**
		⇩												⇩
Terminal Value @SF 70%		⇩		⇩	⇦	⇦	⇦	⇦	⇦	⇦	⇦	⇦	⇦	**110**
Present TV @DR 12.5%		⇩	⇦	**30**										
Present Company Value [mil]		⇩	⇨	**89**										
Sales Multiple				**0.9**										
EBIT Multiple				**7.4**										

Table 1
Business Valuation of an Integrated Service Supplier

Comments:

The great influence of the large base of running contracts as an attenuation factor for the service growth rate is demonstrated by the falling percentaged growth rates as shown in Table 1.

The calculation yields a *sales multiple* of 0.9 and an *EBIT multiple* of 7.4. Both values may appear quite high at first sight. Though, they find their justification in the fact that the business is generating a steady flow of revenues at relatively high profit rates and moderate risks. As already explained, these higher profit rates are the result of less competition in the service for large own installations. In most cases, customers prefer to keep the system suppliers in the loop also for the long-term service of new installations and are prepared to pay a certain premium related to the higher operational risks associated with large and complex systems.

Because the growth of the service business of an installations company depends mainly on the selling of own systems, a valuation of service on a standalone basis is insufficient. It must always be performed in the context of the valuation of the total business which also includes the installations side.

In conclusion, the main source of service growth are own new systems, and protecting the base of running contracts is mission critical. Therefore, the following key aspects are of major relevance in the valuation of an integrated service supplier:

➔ How sustainable is the installations business?

➔ Is service capable of capitalizing on the opportunities stemming from the installation of new systems?

➔ Is service capable of renewing its running contracts?

Regarding the first question, it is important that the installations company regularly wins installation contracts for large and complex systems. For this kind of systems, customers will be more inclined to outsource the service, at least for the first couple of years. It is also important that the company closes its installation projects with good results and receives high customer satisfaction ratings. Good performance in the installation projects is an important prerequisite for starting well into the service of the systems.

The second question covers a couple of aspects related to the market and the strategy of the company. Is the company operating in an outsourcing friendly market, where the majority of customers prefer to engage external suppliers for the service of their systems? The outsourcing maturity for service differs significantly across the different industries. Does the company consider service as an equally important business as the installations one? Does the company have a consistent life-cycle approach (covering the entire life cycle of installations) and how well is the service organization engaged already in the sales process of new systems?

The third question addresses the mission critical aspect of protecting the service contract base. A service business not capable of protecting and renewing its running contracts cannot grow. The loss of important running contracts rarely can be compensated by winning new orders. In this regard, CRM is of major importance. Is there a process in place for assessing the customer satisfaction? How often does the head of service visit important contract sites? A comprehensive life-cycle approach which includes also the modernization of systems is an important additional favorable argument for service companies with regard to retaining their customers.

Valuation of a generic service provider

The valuation of a generic service provider (with no own installations business) will also be demonstrated by means of a hypothetical example based on the following assumptions:

- ➔ Mature company, well established in the market with a proven positive track record in the field of service
- ➔ Outsourcing friendly market

Regarding these two aspects, all comments from the previous example also apply. As in this case there is no installations business, the business mix of installations and service is irrelevant.

Because the service contracts of generic service providers are generally smaller, have a shorter duration (usually 3 years), and are subject to stronger competition (less complex and less proprietary systems), the erosion of the contract base is higher than in the previous example.

For the same reasons, the initial period (number of years) used for calculating the $PV_{(FCF)}$ is shorter than the period used in the previous example. In this case, it is 6 years (twice the average contract duration of 3 years).

The risk categories are the same (operational, contractual, orders, and transfer risk). For generic service providers, the business is not depending on new own installations. It is mainly supported by the renewal of own running contracts and by the acquisition of contracts from other competitors. Additionally, service opportunities for new installations of smaller size and complexity can also be of relevance. Thus, the *orders risk* is primarily related to the capability of taking over contracts from competitors (growth) and the ability to protect the own contract base. The *contractual risk* is comparable to the previous example. The *operational risk* is slightly higher due to several factors such as the unknown technical condition of systems, missing support from the original manufacturers, a lower skills level of service technicians, higher personnel attrition, and high price pressure. Because in the generic service market the lowest price is the main (and often the only) winning argument, suppliers usually calculate their offers 'at the edge'. This implies savings costs by all means without caring too much about project risks.

The *business transfer risk* is significantly lower than in the case of an integrated service supplier. Maintaining smaller systems requires a lower level of skills, and therefore the risk of losing key personnel is reduced. As customers change their service providers frequently, they are less concerned about who the owner of the company is.

Because of the lower complexity of systems, less proprietary components, and shorter contract durations, competition is high. Therefore, the achievable profit rates in this kind of business are significantly lower.

Due to the fact that the long-term development of a generic service company is hard to predict, engaging in the acquisition of such a business entails a high entrepreneurial risk. As in the previous example, this long-term risk will be taken into consideration by introducing a *sustainability factor (SF)* in the calculation of the company's terminal value.
In the case of generic service providers, these long-term risks could be linked to the following aspects:

- ➔ Long-term capability of taking over service contracts from competitors

    - ◆ Does the service provider have a unique value proposition and a competitive advantage?
    - ◆ How fragmented is the service market?

- ➔ Long-term capability of retaining running contracts

    - ◆ Are there any changes expected regarding the general outsourcing maturity of the service market?
    - ◆ How well established is the CRM?
    - ◆ Was the service provider capable of renewing the majority of his running contracts?

The following parameters are used for the valuation presented in Table 2.

Parameter	Value
New Service Business p. a. [mil Euro]	6.0
Erosion Rate Service (ER)	5.0%
Inflation Rate (IR)	2.0%
EBIT Service	7.0%
Discount Rate Service (DR)	11.5%
Risk Free Invest 3.0%	
Operational Risk Service 2.0%	
Contractual Risk Service 1.5%	
Orders Risk 1.5%	
Business Transfer Risk 1.5%	
Inflation 2.0%	
Perpetual Growth Rate Service (GR)	0.5%
Terminal Value Sustainability Factor (SF)	70.0%
Tax Rate (TR)	25.0%

Year			**1**	**2**	**3**	**4**	**5**	**6**	**7**
Service Sales [mil]			100	103	106	109	111	114	117
Additional Business				6.0	6.0	6.0	6.0	6.0	6.0
Service Erosion @-5%				-5.0	-5.2	-5.3	-5.4	-5.6	-5.7
Inflation @2%				2.0	2.1	2.1	2.2	2.2	2.3
Service Growth Rate				3.0%	28.%	2.7%	2.5%	2.4%	2.3%
Service EBIT @EBIT 7%			7.0	7.2	7.4	7.6	7.8	8.0	8.2
Service FCF @25% TAX			**5.3**	**5.4**	**5.6**	**5.7**	**5.9**	**6.0**	**6.1**
			⇩	⇦	⇦	⇦	⇦	⇦	⇩
Present FCF Value @DR 11.5%	⇩	⇦	**23.3**						⇩
	⇩								⇩
Terminal Value @PGR 0.5%	⇩								**55.7**
	⇩								⇩
Terminal Value @ 70% SF	⇩		⇩	⇦	⇦	⇦	⇦	⇦	**39.0**
Present TV @DR 11.5%	⇩	⇦	**18.2**						
Present Company Value [mil]	⇨	⇨	**41.5**						
Sales Multiple			**0.4**						
EBIT Multiple			**5.9**						

Table 2
Business Valuation of a Generic Service Provider

Comments:

In this case, the calculation yields a sales multiple of 0.4 and an EBIT multiple of 5.9. The big difference between the sales multiples (in comparison to the integrated service supplier) is determined by the big difference in the profitability (7% v. 12%).

The main source of growth are contracts which are 'snatched' from other competitors. The new business of 6 mil Euros p. a. corresponds to winning approximately three new contracts of 2 mil each—a typical value for the generic service market and a provider of this size.

Protecting the base of running contracts is mission critical also in this case. Usually, competition in this kind of business is intense and the risk of losing contracts is quite high. Contracts have shorter durations, and customers change their service providers frequently. Succeeding in retaining important contracts over several terms is a strong indicator for the quality of service providers.

Above-mentioned aspects are reflected in the comparatively low growth of the company during the initial period as well as in the low perpetual growth rate.

For generic service providers (who usually service systems of smaller size and less complexity), an EBIT of 7% can be considered as relatively high.

Generic service providers do not have the advantage of profiting from own new installations and proprietary systems. In this kind of business, the lowest price is the main winning argument, and therefore high operational efficiency and a lean administrative structure are important success factors.

Multiples

In the valuation process of businesses, multiples are a frequently used instrument. Nevertheless, they can only provide a vague idea about the business potential of a specific company. A thorough valuation requires determining the fair market value of a business as shown in the above-presented examples. The multiples resulting at the end of this valuation process can be then compared and benchmarked with industry-specific values, if such information exists.

The sales multiple is mainly influenced by the basic profitability of the business. If the profitability doubles, the sales multiple also doubles. The EBIT multiple doesn't change with the basic profitability. A flat business (no growth, no profitability improvement) will yield the same EBIT multiple, regardless if the profitability is 5% or 10%. Both multiples are strongly influenced by the future development of sales and profit: A strong sales growth together with an improvement of the profitability leads to higher multiples. Therefore, multiples condense in one number the view into the future development of a company.

Closing Words

In writing this book, I had two goals in mind. First, I wanted to show systems and installations companies how important service is for their overall success and how to set up service for maximizing its contribution to their business. As mentioned before, building a successful service means regarding it as an equally important business segment as installations and NOT expecting it to come automatically as a residue of the sale of new systems. It also means selecting the best possible people for this job: managers, engineers, and technicians with profound subject matter expertise and a strong dedication to serve their customers. Successful installations companies need to develop a comprehensive life-cycle approach and define their strategy accordingly.
At the same time, it was also my intention to give customers some advice for choosing the right supplier for the service of their installations and to provide them some guidance with regard to establishing a trustful relationship with their service providers.

My other goal was to make service more attractive for young people standing at the beginning of their career. Service is a perfect professional environment for technical specialists as well as for managers. What makes service particularly interesting is the fact that it is a people's business. Especially in the service for large installations, knowledgeable and committed people are the by far most important success factor. In my opinion, leading people is the highest form of management. There is no other technical business where this skill has such a decisive relevance as in service. Only people who combine in their person technical expertise, entrepreneurship, social competence, and empathy can become good service business managers. My advice for all those who think they are such a person is:

"Join the service business. You will not regret it."

Glossary

Systems and installations companies	Companies with the business purpose of designing, engineering, installing, and servicing large systems and installations
Integrated service suppliers	Service organizations belonging to systems and installations companies
Generic service providers	Service organizations of companies offering only service
Resident service (organization)	Service executed by on-site teams inside the premises of the customer's installation
Outsourcing maturity	Tendency of customers in a specific market/industry of executing the service of their installations with external suppliers
Integral O&M	The complete spectrum of maintenance services (corrective, preventive, predictive) and the technical operation of installations. This kind of service requires a resident service organization.
Green-field service	Service provided for new installations going live
Brown-field service	Service provided for old installations (installed base)

Maintenance factor	Annual maintenance costs divided by the asset replacement value of a system
In-house service	Service executed by customers with their own personnel
Control room operations	Services rendered in the control room of a system or installation, like running the system, analyzing operational data, preparing reports, or providing decision support
Field operations	Operational activities carried out in large distributed systems, for example manual encoding and jam busting in airport baggage systems

Appendix

Incentive Scheme

An incentive scheme is an instrument used in performance-based contracts for translating contractual performance into a monetary value. In this regard, any additional payment above the contract base profit is called a bonus, and any deduction from the base profit is called a malus.

Setting up an incentive scheme requires the following steps:

(1) Defining the range in which the monthly/yearly remuneration can vary around the base payment value. For example, the range could be defined at +/- 10%. For a contract with an annual value of 7.2 mil Euros, the monthly payment could thus vary by +/- 60 thousand Euros up and down the base payment of 600 thousand Euros.

(2) Selecting the payment-relevant Key Performance Indicators (KPI). These could be *operational* (e.g. throughput), *technical* (e.g. availability), *financial* (e.g. budget compliance), *quality related* (e.g. compliance regarding the execution of tasks as scheduled in the CMMS), or *soft* indicators (e.g. customer satisfaction scoring). For each indicator, a base (or reference) value and the individual weighting must be defined. Obviously, the sum of all KPI weightings must be 100%.
For example, the base value for the average travel time of bags could be set at 35 minutes and the weighting at 30%. Additionally, for each indicator a maximum performance and a minimum

performance threshold value must be defined. For the 'travel time' KPI, these values could be 25 minutes respectively 40 minutes, with the following meaning: Because the customer cannot make economic use of a travel time of < 25 minutes, the supplier's bonus calculation stops at this value. A bad system performance of above 40 minutes would have to be considered a serious performance issue on the side of the supplier which cannot be handled any longer as just a malus inside the incentive scheme. Such a serious performance issue would not only mean that the supplier's monthly payment is reduced according to the incentive scheme; it usually also means that additional liquidated damages could be applied on top.

(3) For conveying performance into a monetary value, performance credit points are introduced, for example +15 if an individual KPI reaches the maximum performance value, respectively -15 if it drops below the minimum value. Thus, each credit point has a monetary value of (600 t€ * 10%) / 15 = 4t€.

An example of typical KPIs used in the service for airport logistic systems is presented in the following table.

KPI	Name	Unit	Type	Weighting	Base Value	Range (+/-)	Max	Min
1	Left Bags	pcs/1000	O	40%	0.2	15	0.0	0.5
2	Travel Time	min	O	30%	35.0	15	25.0	40.0
3	Availability	%	T	10%	98.5	15	100.0	98.0
4	ATR read rate	%	T	10%	87.0	15	100.0	83.0
5	CMMS compl.	%	Q	10%	95.0	15	100.0	90.0
				100%				

For not making things too complicated, it is recommended that the scheme should be limited to 5 or 6 indicators.

At the end of each reporting period, for example monthly, the current performance values for each KPI are introduced in the 'Current Value' column of the following table. By comparing these values with the respective base and the maximum/minimum performance values (previous table), the (weighted) credit points are calculated for each KPI. With the monetary value of credits points, as previously calculated in paragraph (3), the bonus/malus is then determined. In this example, the supplier earns a bonus on the 'left bags', the 'availability', the 'ATR read rate', and the 'CMMS compliance' KPIs because his performance was above the respective base values. He loses money on the 'travel time' KPI because his performance was below target.

KPI	**Name**	**Unit**	**Current Value**	**Points**	**Weighted Points**	**Bonus/ Malus[t€]**
1	Left Bags	pcs/1000	0.15	3.75	1.50	6.0
2	Travel Time	min	35.20	-0.60	-0.18	-0.7
3	Availability	%	98.90	4.00	0.40	1.6
4	ATR read rate	%	90.00	3.46	0.35	1.4
5	CMMS compliance	%	98.00	9.00	0.90	3.6
					2.97	**11.9**

The bonus, in this example 11.9 thousand Euros, is added on top of the supplier's base monthly payment of 600 thousand Euros, yielding a total payment of 611.9 thousand Euros.

Above-methodology can be easily implemented in a spreadsheet. With such a tool, the supplier's performance and his payment can be documented and calculated is a systematic, easy to handle, and comprehensible manner.